SAINTS

WHO BATTLED

SATAN

SAINTS
WHO BATTLED
SATAN

Seventeen Holy Warriors
Who Can Teach You How to Fight the Good Fight
and Vanquish Your Ancient Enemy

Paul Thigpen

TAN Books
Charlotte, North Carolina

Cover images: Gustave Dore and *The Temptation of St. Anthony* (engraving), Schongauer, Martin (1440-91) / Bibliotheque Nationale, Paris, France / Peter Willi / Bridgeman Images

Book and cover design by David Ferris
www.davidferrisdesign.com

ISBN: 978-1-61890-718-9

Cataloging-in-Publication data on file with the Library of Congress

Printed and bound in the United States of America

TAN Books
Charlotte, North Carolina
www.TANBooks.com
2015

For my daughter, Lydia; her husband,
Michael; and my son, Elijah

"Fight the good fight of the faith!"
1 Timothy 6:12

St. Michael the archangel, defend us in battle. Be our protection against the wickedness and snares of the Devil. May God rebuke him, we humbly pray, and do thou, O prince of the heavenly host, by the power of God thrust into hell Satan and all the evil spirits who prowl about the world seeking the ruin of souls. AMEN.

—POPE LEO XIII

– CONTENTS –

– INTRODUCTION –

OUR COMRADES, THE SAINTS
The Church Triumphant and
the Church Militant

The life of man upon the earth is a warfare.
Tobit 12:13 (Douay-Rheims)

A century and a half before the coming of Christ, the Jewish homeland was invaded, occupied, and desecrated by troops of the Seleucid Empire. Judas Maccabeus was the Jewish general who led his followers in armed resistance to the foreigners and their attempts to force the Jews to abandon their faith.

Before one of their battles, Judas exhorted the soldiers to fight valiantly. "He armed each of them," the Scripture tells us, "not so much with confidence in shields and spears as with the inspiration of brave words, and he cheered them all by relating a dream, a sort of vision, which was worthy of belief" (2 Mc 15:11).

In this vision, the general saw Onias, a former high priest, "praying with outstretched arms for the whole body of the Jews" (v. 12). Then he saw the prophet Jeremiah, "who loves the brethren and prays much for the people and the holy city." The prophet was a man of "marvelous majesty and authority" (v. 14).

1

Both of these men had died some time before Judas received the vision. But by their prayers, they were helping their brothers still on earth who needed comrades in the struggle—not just for their homeland, but for their souls. The vision concluded with a scene guaranteed to fortify the faith of the soldiers: "Jeremiah stretched out his right hand and gave to Judah a golden sword, and as he gave it, he addressed him thus: 'Take this holy sword, a gift from God, with which you will strike down your adversaries'" (vv. 15-16).

The battle soon began, and the Jewish resistance fighters were victorious.

The Devil Prowls

This vision of Judas should serve us even today as a consolation and an inspiration. We too are engaged in a critical battle for our souls—and ours is fought against the ancient and powerful Enemy of all the human race. "Be sober, be watchful," St. Peter warns. "Your adversary the Devil prowls around like a roaring lion, seeking someone to devour" (1 Pt 5:8).

Thanks be to God that we have as our comrades in this conflict a host of saints in heaven. Now that they have won their own battle and their victor's crown, they stand before God, sharing in the triumph of Jesus Christ their Commander, who vanquished Satan on the Cross. But they are by no means simply resting on their laurels in God's presence. As members of the Church Triumphant (those who can now exult in victory), they are eager to assist the members of the Church Militant (those who must still soldier on in this world).

Their courageous conduct when they too were soldiers on earth can provide us with a marvelous example to follow. Because they knew how to fight and defeat the Devil, their wisdom can advise us. Best of all, they now have a share in

God's own nature (see 2 Pt 1:4), which includes His power and authority: "If we persevere, we shall also reign with Him" (2 Tm 2:12). So they are able not just to intercede for us but to engage the Enemy directly and effectively on our behalf through the divine power that they share.

Together, under the leadership of Christ, our Commander, the Church Triumphant and the Church Militant make up a mighty army (with the angels, of course, as its third division). The twelfth-century mystical writer Hugh of St. Victor describes this reality vividly:

> For the Incarnate Word is our King, who came into this world to war with the Devil. . . . The king himself is in the midst of His army and proceeds protected and surrounded on all sides by His columns. . . . All are serving the one King and following the one banner. All are pursuing the one enemy and are being crowned by the one victory.[1]

Why Were These Particular Saints Chosen?

The purpose of this book is to present the stories and insights of a number of saints who battled Satan so that we can become more familiar with our heavenly comrades and more eager to seek their help. From among the many saints I could have included, I have chosen a few, presented in chronological order, whose experience offers a wide variety of compelling lessons in combat. I have not attempted to provide a biography of each saint but only enough information to identify them and to tell about their struggles.

In each chapter, I have also tried to present a bit of historical context that notes the features of the broader spiritual battlefield of the Church of that time. My hope is that such context serves as a reminder that our warfare is not just a matter of personal interior struggle, and that the conduct

---

[1] Hugh of St. Victor, *On the Sacraments of the Christian Faith*, II.

of each spiritual soldier makes a critical difference in the outcome of the wider battle.

In many ways, the accounts in this book can be seen as historical illustrations of the spiritual realities and principles laid out in my *Manual for Spiritual Warfare* (TAN Books, 2014). There, I offer a brief summary of Satan's strategies, as well as the weapons and armor we have been given by God to defeat him.

In the present work, we can see concrete examples of how the Devil assaults his foes, not just through extraordinary preternatural attacks but through common temptations, both powerful and subtle. We can observe how the saints have used prayer and fasting, the sacraments, sacramentals, the Scripture, and other spiritual weapons to resist him. And we can discover how the virtues they cultivated protected their souls as a sturdy armor against diabolical temptation and attack.

"Worthy of Belief"

Skeptics may read these accounts and scoff in disbelief. Perhaps they deny the existence of demons or presume that preternatural phenomena simply do not occur. Even so, my personal experiences and those of countless others—not to mention the testimony of Our Lord Himself, Scripture, and two millennia of Christian tradition—have all convinced me otherwise.

I present these stories, then, for the same reason that Judas told his soldiers about his vision: They are powerful and heartening, and I consider them "worthy of belief" (2 Mc 15:11). My prayer, then, is that in reading such remarkable accounts of saints who battled Satan, "inspired by them you may wage the good warfare, holding faith and a good conscience" (1 Tm 1:18–19).

Paul Thigpen
August 4, 2015
Feast of St. John Vianney

- CHAPTER 1 -

EVE AND THE SERPENT
The War Begins

And the great dragon was thrown down, that ancient
serpent, who is called the Devil and Satan, the deceiver
of the whole world—he was thrown down to the earth,
and his angels were thrown down with him.

Revelation 12:9

She was utterly innocent, untainted by sin, unacquainted with misery. But she was also untested, so her innocence left her gullible, vulnerable to the wiles of a deadly Enemy masquerading as her friend.

Her name was Eve. And her Enemy's name was Satan.

Eve and her husband, Adam, were of course the first parents of the human race. They were created by God in His own image, with an intellect and a free will, as a beloved son and daughter who could love Him in return. They walked with God in righteousness—that is, in right relationship with Him, with each other, with themselves, and with the world that God had given them to be their home.

They lived in Eden, a paradise, free from disordered desires, suffering, sorrow, and death. They had received divine grace as a supernatural gift to unite them to God. And they possessed the knowledge and wisdom necessary to achieve the destiny that God had appointed for them: to love, serve, enjoy, and glorify Him forever.

Angelic Rebellion

Satan, on the other hand, was an angel. He had been created a pure spirit by God, good and splendid with the gifts that God had given him and his fellow angels so that they, too, might achieve their appointed destiny. His name was originally Lucifer, the "light bearer." He was mighty and brilliant and beautiful.

But Satan had rejected that destiny. He had chosen instead his own defiant path in an attempt to overthrow his Creator and take His place. Many of his angelic comrades had followed his lead.

How, we might ask, could a few grains of sand on the seashore ever hope to subdue the ocean? How could a swarm of gnats think to rule the sky? Their pride had darkened their minds, and they had deceived themselves.

Their judgment was swift and sure. The angels still loyal to God cast them out of heaven, with the Archangel Michael leading the battle against the fallen ones.

These unclean spirits, now the Devil and his demons, had no possibility of repentance and reform. The free and full choice they had made with all their being was definitive, irrevocable. They could never return home.

Their hatred toward God knew no bounds. Since they could not conquer Him, they would vent their rage by assaulting His children, defiling His image. And whenever possible, they would draw His sons and daughters down with them into the hellfire of absolute, eternal separation from their Father in heaven.

When the time was right, then, the Devil slithered as a serpent into the garden of paradise. The war in heaven had become a war on earth.

Seductions, Lies, and Doubts

What would be the Adversary's strategy? First, divide and conquer. When the woman was alone, he would come to her. And once he had overcome her, he would go for her husband, through her. He would not approach them together; together, they would have more strength to resist.

When Satan found Eve, he spoke smoothly, gently, not with a threat or even a challenge, but with a probe posing as a reasonable question. "Did God say, 'You shall not eat of any tree of the garden?'" (Gn 3:1).

She replied that God had said they could eat the fruit of all the trees except one: the tree of the knowledge of good and evil. If they ate from that tree, or even touched it, God had warned they would die (see Gn 3:2–3).

Clearly, she knew the divine commandment. So the Devil's task would be to entice her to disobey it knowingly. If she did, she would be joining him in his rebellion.

He knew just the trick.

First, Satan planted doubts in her mind about God's character and intentions. "You will not die," he insisted (Gn 3:4). *God is a liar.* "For God knows that when you eat of it, your eyes will be opened, and you will be like God, knowing good and evil" (v. 5). *God sees you as a rival. He wants to keep you from becoming a threat to His power.*

The oily thoughts greased her mind, so that her faith in God began to slip away.

"You will be like God." The words resonated within her powerfully, for they echoed her deepest longing. After all, God had made her in His own image; He had *created* her to be like Him. No wonder she felt drawn to that tree.

"The woman saw that the tree was good for food, and that it was a delight to the eyes, and that the tree was to be desired to make one wise" (Gn 3:6). The Enemy was crafty. He pointed out to her the attractive things that she naturally desired, because they were good in themselves: likeness to God, nourishing food, beauty, wisdom. Then he suggested a shortcut to obtain those goods: disobedience to God.

Eve surrendered, it seems, without a fight. She ate the fruit and gave it to Adam. He surrendered as well. They lost the battle almost as soon as it had begun.

A World of Woe

The new prisoners were dragged into the Enemy's camp, naked and trembling, full of fear and shame. God's judgment followed swiftly, as each one tried to escape the sentence by passing the blame: "The woman whom You gave to be with me, she gave me fruit of the tree, and I ate" (Gn 3:12). "The Serpent beguiled me, and I ate" (v. 13).

A divine curse sealed their fate: Pain and sorrow, toil and trouble would be their miserable lot. Just as they had rebelled against God, their bodies would rebel against their souls, and the earth would rebel against their stewardship, until death came at last—relief, yes, but a terrifying relief.

Even so, in the gathering darkness, a single spark of hope appeared. God prophesied that the day would come when the Seed of the woman—her descendant—would crush the head of the Serpent (see Gn 3:15). For thousands of years, the recollection of those puzzling words would provoke countless debates about their meaning.

Yet one thing was certain. Though the first battle had been lost, the war on earth had only just begun.

CHAPTER 2

THE BLESSED VIRGIN MARY
Queen of Angels, Bane of Devils
(First Century)

He who is mighty has done great things for me, and holy is His name. . . . He has shown strength with His arm, He has scattered the proud in the imagination of their hearts, He has put down the mighty from their thrones, and exalted those of low degree.
Luke 9:49, 51–52

She was utterly innocent, untainted by sin, though acquainted with sorrow. The ancient Enemy pursued her, but he could get no hold on her (see Rv 12:13–16). For she was full of grace, and God preserved her from sin (see Lk 1:28).

Her name was Mary. She was the new Eve. Her obedience to God would be the mighty sword that cut the tangled knot once tied by the disobedience of the first Eve.

Millennia had passed since the primal tragedy in paradise. The Serpent's head was not yet crushed, and his venom had spread throughout the earth. Millions of the descendants of Eden's exiles had been taken prisoner, and many had become traitors and collaborators, joining the ranks of their evil conqueror.

But over the centuries, God had slowly revealed His battle plan. His stirring call went out for warriors who would remain brave and loyal in the fray, even when they were weak and wounded. And His call was answered by some in every generation.

On the Front Lines

It was two thousand years ago that one of the angels still loyal to God appeared to Mary to call her to war. It was not a call simply to defensive measures—to resist the Devil's temptations. No, the grace-filled virtues of her soul provided her an armor that he was never able to penetrate that way.

Instead, she was called to storm the gates of hell. This humble, unassuming young maiden would take her place on the front lines of the battle. She would face off with the Prince of Darkness himself as she stood shining in the radiant power of the Almighty, the Most High God (see Lk 1:35).

How would Mary be able to fulfill such a destiny? She was summoned to become the Mother of God so that her divine Son might bring to pass the ancient prophecy. Taking her flesh to become a Man, He could fight and conquer the Enemy on behalf of mankind. But His divine Father first sought her consent to take that singular, and singularly costly, role.

She humbly embraced the message: "Behold, I am the handmaid of the Lord. Let it be to me according to Your word" (Lk 1:38).

In that moment, "the Word became flesh and dwelt among us" (Jn 1:14). Jesus Christ was conceived, the Commander in Chief of a new, invincible army. In a daring act of humility beyond all imagination, of love beyond the telling, the Son of God pitched His tent on the battlefield of this miserable planet—knowing that the price of victory would be His very lifeblood.

Mother of Sorrows

Before long, the ancient Serpent—now a ravenous Dragon driven by bloodlust—sprang into action. He could not fully predict his Adversary's strategy, because he could not fathom the divine humility nor understand the divine love. But he knew enough to realize that this woman's Child would "rule . . . with a rod of iron" (Rv 12:5), and the rod was meant to crush his own diabolical head.

If he could not tempt the mother, then he would murder her Child—and drown her soul in grief. His first brutal attempt, the slaughter of the innocents of Bethlehem, failed. So the Dragon made long-term plans for a future assault. But in the meantime, he turned his fury upon Mary. She would never be a sinful mother, but he would make sure she would be a sorrowful mother.

Simeon's prophecy in the temple, telling of a sword that would pierce her heart, was only the beginning of her grief (see Lk 2:35). When the neighbors claimed that Mary was crazy or, worse yet, an adulteress; when the boy Jesus was lost in Jerusalem; when He left her home alone to begin His ministry; when His enemies condemned Him as a blasphemer, called Him a demon-possessed fraud, tried to throw Him off a cliff—the Dragon whispered, incessantly, his darkest threats, seeking to provoke Mary's deepest fears.

But despite her torment, she remained steadfast, a tower of ivory. Her soul was a hidden garden where she communed with her Lord and drew from His strength. The ancient Foe, she knew, could advance no farther than divine providence permitted. So her declaration to heaven remained: "Let it be to me according to your word." In His own time, God would scatter "the proud in the imagination of their hearts" (Lk 1:51).

Mary's Armor

Then, at last, the hour came for the Prince of Darkness to have his murderous way (see Lk 22:53). Imagine the scene: He slithers around her feet at the foot of her Son's cross. As she watches the Heart of her heart hang there in exquisite agony, the Enemy whispers, "I have conquered. His mission, and your mission, have failed. He will be food for the worms."

It seems that all is lost. But Mary is a queen, and a war-rior queen. "He who is mighty has done great things" for her, and His mercy and strength will prevail (see Lk 1:49–51).

She wears "the whole armor of God . . . to stand against the wiles of the Devil" (Eph 6:11). The truth about her Son and His mission is firmly fastened around her waist. Her righ-teousness is a breastplate to protect her heart. The shield of her enduring faith quenches all the darts of the Evil One. The firm conviction that God is her Savior (see Lk 1:47) is a helmet that protects her mind from the Enemy's lies (see Eph 6:14–17).

She recalls God's word to her so many years before—that her Son is a King who will "reign . . . forever" (Lk 1:33). So she takes up that word as a sword against the ancient Foe (Eph 6:17). Her feet are shod with the gospel of peace, soaked by the precious Blood of Jesus that has trickled down upon them from the Cross, the eternal Sacrifice that will finally reconcile the world to God.

As her Son shouts His final war cry—"It is finished!" (*The mission is accomplished! The victory is won!*)—the Serpent rears up his ugly head from the stony ground in one last attempt to terrorize her.

But she looks him in the eye, lifts up her blood-stained foot, and crushes his head.

Demons Tremble at Her Name

In the days that followed such a glorious triumph, Mary's faith and fortitude were royally rewarded: Her Son rose from the dead and ascended to His heavenly throne. There He ruled again at His Father's right hand.

She longed to follow Him there. But the Church He had established on earth needed just a little longer her tangible wit-ness, her wisdom, and her example—for the Enemy, though defeated, was allowed to test them in battle until the day when her Son would return to earth and cast him into prison forever.

When the time came at last for her reunion with her Son, He refused to take her soul alone but carried her body as well to a place at His side. His own flesh, now glorified, He had received from her flesh; He would not leave it to decay in the earth. There she received, from both the angels and the redeemed souls, the honor and praise fitting for the Queen Mother of the King of the Universe.

Even so, she could not forget the plight of her children still on earth, the children Jesus had given her while He was dying (see Jn 19:26–27). Just as He was interceding for them at the Father's right hand (see Rom 8:34), she would intercede for them at her Son's right hand. And as the angels were now under her command, she would dispatch them to enter the fray on earth on behalf of those who sought her assistance.

The demons learned to tremble at her name. As one of her great devotees, St. Bonaventure, would one day observe, "Men do not fear a powerful, hostile army as much as the powers of hell fear the name and protection of Mary."

The Queen of Angels had become the bane of devils.

- CHAPTER 3 -

ST. JOSEPH
Terror of Demons
(First Century)

*An angel of the Lord appeared to Joseph in a dream
and said, "Rise, take the Child and His mother, and flee
to Egypt, and remain there till I tell you; for Herod is
about to search for the Child, to destroy Him."*
Matthew 2:13

Our Father in heaven could have chosen any man on earth to be the guardian of His beloved Son and the husband of the Child's mother. We can imagine His criteria for the role.

First, the man had to be holy. He would be married to a sinless woman and rearing a sinless Son, joined to them in a love beyond measure. She needed a holy companion, and the Boy needed a holy role model.

Second, God sought a good provider, a diligent and skilled worker who could earn enough to care for them properly. Even if their food, clothing, and shelter would be modest, it would be honestly earned. And to make the most of God's provision in challenging situations, he would need to be resourceful, able to find shelter in a stable when the inn was full, and turn a manger into a crib for a newborn Babe.

A holy man, a good provider—this was the kind of man that God sought. But the man had to be that and much more. He had to be a mighty warrior as well.

The Holy Family would be a little city under perpetual siege by the ancient Foe. Who would be chosen to guard the city walls?

Joseph, "a Just Man"

God chose St. Joseph. He was "a just man" (Mt 1:19), a holy man, and a hard-working, resourceful carpenter. And when the Enemy launched assaults against his family, the armor of his character and the weapons of his righteous conduct were their sure defense.

When Joseph learned that Mary was carrying a Child who was not his, no doubt the Devil's thoughts came furiously: *Adulteress! She deserves to be publicly shamed and shunned! No—she should be stoned!* But Joseph's kindness was Mary's shield, and he sought instead to send her away quietly, far from wagging tongues and scornful glances.

Then, when the angel appeared in Joseph's dreams to tell him to wed Mary and take the Child as his own, Satan most surely would have sought to plant doubts that God had spoken, just as he had in Eden. *Has God really said to keep that woman? How could her Child be conceived by the Holy Spirit? Blasphemy! Send her away as she deserves!*

But Joseph stood firm in his confidence that God had spoken and that God speaks only the truth. He would bravely endure the whispered rumors, the open taunts, the mockery of his manhood that would surely come. He received the heavenly instructions in faith, just as Mary had done.

They both had made the words of the prophet their own: "I have set my face like flint, and I know that I shall not be put to shame; He who vindicates me is near" (Is 50:7–8). Together they faced the Enemy and stared him in the face. God was at their side, and they would obey Him at all costs.

The Slaughter of the Innocents

Satan was no doubt furious. Presenting Mary and Joseph with temptations of anger, doubt, and fear had been futile; the situation called for stronger measures. He would launch a violent, murderous assault on the Child and those who tried to protect Him. And the Devil knew just how to make it happen.

Herod was a vain, arrogant, ambitious politician—and powerful. What provocations might the Enemy have stirred up in his heart when the Magi spoke of a newborn King in Bethlehem? *This Child is your rival. You must assassinate Him immediately. Do whatever it takes.*

Herod was also ruthless. He had a history of brutality toward those he viewed as threats, having murdered even members of his own family. So the screams of babies and their mothers who were strangers in far-off Bethlehem mattered little to him.

The king ordered the massacre of the innocents. The Dragon was confident he would devour the Child who would rule the nations (see Rv 12:4–5), but he had not counted on Joseph's mighty faith and invincible obedience.

Once again, heaven spoke. "Rise, take the Child and His mother, and flee" (Mt 2:13). Once again, Joseph listened, believed, and obeyed immediately. But how many diabolical doubts rose up to threaten his mind like a flood?

What prudent man would set off for a foreign country in the middle of the night? How foolish, how dangerous, to go without proper provisions, without alerting your families! The highway to Egypt is long and desolate and treacherous, crawling with snakes and scorpions and robbers. All this because of a dream?

Doubtful hesitation would have been deadly. But Joseph's instant, faith-filled obedience thwarted the Enemy's siege of the Holy Family. They escaped to safety.

Terror of Demons

We can be confident that Joseph's righteous character and behavior continued to serve, all the days of his life, as a defense for his beloved wife and foster Son. Whatever attacks the ancient Foe may have attempted in the "hidden years" of the Holy Family at Nazareth, those attacks were unsuccessful, surely in large part because of Joseph's protection. He was a man who could confidently declare with his forefather David, "Let God arise, let His enemies be scattered!" (Ps 68:1).

After Joseph left this world for the next, he went on to take on the mantle of a defender, not just of the Holy Family but of the extended family of Jesus and Mary—that is, the whole Church. Many titles ascribed to him in the litany that bears his name remind us of this role: Guardian of Virgins, Pillar of Families, Patron of the Dying, Protector of the Holy Church. But none among them is more fitting than the title that reveals his might as a spiritual warrior: *Terror of Demons*.

Joseph may well have been a man of few words. Sacred Scripture has recorded nothing from his lips. But this title reminds us that when we call on him for rescue from our diabolical adversaries, he need not even speak to them: His very presence terrifies them and sends them fleeing.

- CHAPTER 4 -

ST. PAUL
Harassed by an Angel of Satan
(Died c. 67)

And to keep me from being too elated by the abundance of revelations, a thorn was given me in the flesh, a messenger of Satan, to harass me, to keep me from being too elated. Three times I begged the Lord about this, that it should leave me; but He said to me, "My grace is sufficient for you, for My power is made perfect in weakness."

2 Corinthians 12:7-8

He was a man of brilliant intellect, impeccable credentials, and uncommon religious zeal. "As to righteousness under the Law," he once boasted, he was "blameless" (Phil 3:6). But his superior qualities led him to pride, and pride gave birth to fear and hatred.

His name was Saul, and he was among the fiercest persecutors of the first Christians. Utterly self-assured in his religious practice, with absolute confidence in his interpretation of Scripture, he felt justified in terrorizing the new believers who held novel teachings. When one of their leaders was stoned to death by a mob, he watched with satisfaction.

Eventually, Saul went so far as to hunt down Christians in their homes, drag them away in chains, and throw them in jail. The same demonic forces that had inspired the murderers of Jesus were now seeking to annihilate His followers, and Saul became part of that diabolical plot. His mind and

heart were darkened and twisted with violent rage. Yet into
the bitter darkness there came one day a blinding light.

"Breathing threats and murder against the disciples of
the Lord" (Acts 9:1), Saul set out from Jerusalem to the city
of Damascus. His goal was to arrest the Christians there and
bring them back to prison. But God had other plans.

As this self-appointed religious sheriff approached
Damascus, a brilliant light from heaven flashed around
him. He fell to the ground in helpless terror and heard the
voice of Jesus confront him. "Saul, Saul, why do you persecute Me?"

"Who are you, Lord?"

"I am Jesus, whom you are persecuting; but rise and
enter the city, and you will be told what you are to do" (Acts
9:4–6).

With that burning, cleansing, liberating beam of radiance, Saul's pride was humbled, his hatred was neutralized,
and his soul was set free of the Enemy's control. He stood
up, and though his physical eyes were temporarily blinded,
his spiritual eyes could finally see. Satan had lost another
soldier, and this one had the makings of a general.

Commissioned and Deployed

Immediately Saul prepared for his commissioning. He took
up the spiritual weapons of prayer and fasting for three days
to battle the demons who were desperately trying to win him
back. When a Christian of Damascus, Ananias, followed
divine instructions to lay hands on Saul and pray for him,
Saul was healed of his bodily blindness and filled with the
Holy Spirit.

Right away, the new convert was baptized. In that life-
giving sacrament, he was cleansed of his sins, "delivered . . .
from the dominion of darkness and transferred . . . to the
kingdom of [God's] beloved Son" (Col 1:13). In only a matter of days, Saul—now known as Paul—was pushing back the

forces of darkness in the strength of Jesus Christ, his new Commander (see Acts 9:17-22).

The Devil, that father of lies, had been deceiving Paul's people, leading them to reject Christ as their promised Savior and the Son of God. But Paul's thundering voice challenged the deception and brought many to the truth. Once, when a sorcerer tried to prevent Paul's preaching through his diabolical craft, Paul called down the power of God against the deceiver and stopped him immediately (see Acts 13:4-12).

Demonic powers that had once provoked Paul to assault the Christians now stirred up violent mobs against him as well. Countless times, he was savagely beaten, including three times with wooden rods. Once he was even stoned and left for dead. Five times he received thirty-nine lashes, one less than the forty prescribed as a death sentence by flogging (see Acts 14:19; 16:23; 21:31-32; 2 Cor 11:25).

But despite the brutal battering, Paul soldiered on, launching his own counteroffensive against the powers of darkness.

Apostolic Authority

Called by Jesus Christ to be an apostle, Paul had received the apostolic authority to cast demons out of those who were possessed (see Mt 28:18-20; Mk 16:15). In the name of Jesus, he was able to perform both healings and exorcisms. Divine power flowed through him abundantly. When handkerchiefs and aprons touched to his body were laid on the sick and possessed, the illnesses were cured and the demons fled in terror (see Acts 19:11-12).

A striking incident from those days demonstrates the notoriety that Paul had achieved among the hosts of darkness. Seven men without Christ's authority to perform exorcisms—men who weren't even Christians—had observed the powerful effects of the Apostle's ministry in the name of Jesus. When they attempted to cast out a demon by imitating

Paul, the evil spirit snarled at them: "Jesus I know; and Paul I know; but who are you?" (Acts 19:15).

"And the man in whom the evil spirit was leaped on them, mastered all of them, and overpowered them, so that they fled out of that house naked and wounded" (v. 16). This frightening incident became the talk of the town, sobering Paul's opponents and encouraging his supporters. As a result, many who had opened themselves to demonic influences by practicing sorcery came to realize that the powers of darkness were no match for Jesus Christ. They repented of their desire to manipulate others through occult powers, publicly burning the books they had used to practice the craft.

A Messenger of Satan

A puzzling comment Paul once made in writing to the Corinthian Christians has fueled scriptural debates ever since. Having told them about certain mystical revelations he had received from heaven, he noted that "a thorn was given [him] in the flesh"—a certain persistent difficulty that dogged him, to keep him from getting puffed up with pride. He called it "a messenger of Satan" or, more literally, "an *angel* of Satan" (2 Cor 12:7).

No one today knows for sure what exactly Paul was talking about. Speculations about the nature of the "thorn" have ranged widely: a physical ailment or disability, chronic depression or some other psychological problem, a difficult social relation, haunting memories of his past as a persecutor of the Church. The words "angel of Satan" might even indicate that it was a demonic power allowed to harass him in some way.

Whatever the exact nature of the adversity, Paul's comment suggests that he recognized the Devil's involvement in it. And that leaves us with a dilemma: How could this man who exercised powerful apostolic authority over the demons be subject to enduring harassment from the Enemy?

The Apostle himself tells us how it could be: God allowed the "thorn" to keep him humble. And God allowed the "thorn" to remain to remind him of his dependence on divine grace: "Three times I begged the Lord about this, that it should leave me; but He said to me, 'My grace is sufficient for you, for My power is made perfect in weakness.' I will all the more gladly boast of my weaknesses, that the power of Christ may rest upon me" (2 Cor 12:8-9).

Several centuries later, St. Augustine would observe that "as an artist, God makes use even of the Devil." The bright colors in a painting, he reasoned, stand out most clearly when viewed beside the dark ones.

In the life of Paul, the Lord was creating a masterpiece of grace. So he permitted the Prince of Darkness to cast a shadow there, allowing the light of heaven to appear more radiant still.

Mission Accomplished

After many years of spiritual combat, Paul's mission was accomplished, and his Commander called him home. Writing to his young disciple St. Timothy, the aging warrior declared, "The time of my departure has come. I have fought the good fight, I have finished the race, I have kept the faith" (2 Tm 4:6-7).

In those days, war heroes returning home received crowns to recognize their victories. Paul had a firm hope that his was awaiting him in heaven: "From now on there is laid up for me the crown of righteousness, which the Lord, the righteous judge, will award to me on that day" (v. 8).

The final assault by the Devil came, according to ancient tradition, around A.D. 67. At that time, the evil emperor Nero—a demon-driven man if ever there was one—had Paul beheaded. But the soldier's faith remained firm to the end as he faced his homecoming: "The Lord will rescue me from every evil and save me for His heavenly kingdom," Paul declared. "To Him be the glory for ever and ever. Amen" (2 Tm 3:18).

Of course, St. Paul was not the only victim of Nero's wrath. This insanely wicked emperor had St. Peter crucified upside down, and he unleashed on the Christians at Rome a fierce persecution whose horrors must have delighted the demons.

Consider just one example of his diabolical attacks on the Church: After their arrest and torture, many Christians were wrapped in cloth that had been soaked in pitch and other highly flammable materials. Then they were bound or nailed to wooden stakes erected in the emperor's gardens. When his guests arrived to enjoy his dinner parties, the Christians were set afire to serve as lanterns to illuminate the festivities.

Could the inspiration to perpetrate such savagery have come from anywhere but hell?

- CHAPTER 5 -

ST. PERPETUA
Spiritual Gladiator
(Died c. 203)

For we are not contending against flesh and blood, but against the principalities, against the powers, against the world rulers of this present darkness, against the spiritual hosts of wickedness in the heavenly places.
Ephesians 6:11-12

Nero's terrors were only the first of the Roman imperial persecutions orchestrated by Satan. Beginning in his reign, to be a Christian was made a crime punishable by death, though pardon could be obtained if a believer publicly renounced Christ and paid honor to the pagan gods. Nine major persecutions by various emperors were to follow, with many assaults on the Church focused on a particular region.

The fifth major persecution, under the emperor Septimus Severus, took place in the early years of the third century. In the Roman province of North Africa, the demons had stirred up among the local pagans considerable animosity against the Christians. Around the year 203, in the great city of Carthage, a group of catechumens was arrested—those who were receiving instruction to enter the Church but had not yet been baptized.

Among them was Perpetua, a married noblewoman about twenty-two years old, who was still nursing her infant son. She and the others were able to arrange for a hurried baptism before their confinement. The graces of that sacrament rescued them from the dominion of darkness and helped prepare them for the spiritual contest that lay ahead.[1]

The Devil Tempts Through Her Father

The new Christians were cast into the dark and filthy dungeon beneath the prison, surrounded and intimidated by bestial imperial guards. No doubt the Enemy whispered disturbing thoughts into Perpetua's mind: images of the horrible fate that awaited her, sounds of her orphaned baby screaming alone.

Yet more troubling still, and more potent, were the words spoken by her dear father but inspired by the Enemy. He was a pagan, and unwittingly, he became the instrument of the Devil's temptation. In the prison diary she left behind, Perpetua described the terrible sadness she felt because she had to grieve and disobey her father for the sake of her Lord:

> Because of his affection for me, my father pressed doggedly to turn me aside and to cast me down from the faith. "Father," I said, "do you see, let's say, that the vessel lying here is a little pitcher? Or is it something else?"
>
> He replied, "I can see that it's a pitcher."
>
> So I asked him, "Can it be called by any other name than what it truly is?"
>
> "No," he replied.

---

[1] This account is based on the third-century text known as *The Martyrdom of Perpetua and Felicitas*, which contains the prison diary of St. Perpetua and material from several of her contemporaries. Quoted dialogue is adapted from the translation by R. E. Wallis that appears in an appendix of Alexander Roberts and James Robertson, eds., *The Ante-Nicene Fathers: The Writings of the Fathers Down to* A.D. *325* (repr., Grand Rapids, Mich.: William B. Eerdmans, 1986), vol. III, *Latin Christianity: Its Founder, Tertullian*, 699–706, par. 5–11.

"Then neither can I call myself anything other than what I am: a Christian."

My father, provoked by what I said, threw himself on me, as if he would tear out my eyes. But he only saddened me. So he went away, overcome by the arguments of the Devil.[2]

Satan's work through her grieving father did not end there. On the day she and her companions were summoned from the prison to appear before the tribunal, he showed up to beg her again to save her life by renouncing her Lord.

"Have pity, my daughter, on my gray hairs. Have pity on your father, if I am worthy to be called a father by you. If with these hands I have brought you up to this flower of your age, if I have preferred you to all your brothers, don't deliver me up to the scorn of men. Think of your brothers, think of your mother and your aunt, think of your son, who won't be able to survive after you die.

"Lay aside your courage; don't bring us all to destruction. For none of us will be able to speak in freedom if you should suffer anything."

These things my father said in his affection, kissing my hands, and throwing himself at my feet; and with tears he called me not "Daughter," but "Lady." And I grieved over the gray hairs of my father, that he alone of all my family would not rejoice over my passion. And I comforted him, saying, "On that scaffold whatever God wills shall happen. For know that we are not placed in our own power, but in that of God."

And he departed from me in sorrow.[3]

Yet a third time her father appeared when Perpetua and the others were arraigned before the procurator, Hilarianus,

---

[2] *Martyrdom*, I, 2.

[3] *Martyrdom*, II, 3.

who had the power to sentence them to death if they refused to deny Christ. This time the elderly man had her infant son in his arms. "Have pity on your baby!" he cried out.

The prosecutor implored her: "Spare the gray hairs of your father, spare the infancy of your boy: Offer sacrifice for the well-being of the emperors."

She replied, "I won't do it."

So Hilarianus asked, "Are you a Christian?"

She answered firmly, "I am a Christian."

Her confession sealed her fate. She was sentenced, along with the others, to face the wild beasts in the arena for the entertainment of the mob.

Then the procurator ordered that her father be beaten with rods as she watched. "My father's misfortune grieved me as if I myself had been beaten," she recorded in her journal, "because I grieved so deeply for his miserable old age." [4]

Finally, when the day of her execution was near, her father came to her one last time. Worn out with suffering, he began to tear out his beard and throw himself to the ground on his face. He cried out, lamenting that in his old age he should suffer such a fate and saying "such words as might move all creation." [5] But all Perpetua could do was to grieve that his last years should be filled with such unhappiness.

Treading Upon the Dragon

While in the dungeon, at her brother's request, Perpetua asked God to show her whether she and her companions would suffer the threatened sentence or somehow escape it. In response, she received a stirring and profound vision of the spiritual combat to come.

> I saw a golden ladder of marvelous height, reaching up to heaven and very narrow, so that people could ascend

---

[4] *Martyrdom*, II, 1.
[5] *Martyrdom*, III, 1.

it only one at a time. On the sides of the ladder were fastened every kind of iron weapon. There were swords, lances, hooks, daggers; so that if anyone climbed up carelessly, or failed to look upwards, he would be torn to pieces and his flesh would cleave to the iron weapons.

Under the ladder itself was crouching a Dragon of amazing size, who lay in wait for those who ascended and frightened them away from making the ascent. And Saturus [one of the Christians who had already been martyred] went up first. . . . He reached the top of the ladder and turned toward me, saying, "Perpetua, I'm waiting for you; but be careful that the Dragon doesn't bite you."

I said, "In the name of the Lord Jesus Christ, he shall not hurt me." Then from under the ladder itself, as if in fear of me, the Dragon slowly lifted up his head; and as I took the first step, I stepped upon his head. Then I went up, and I saw an immense garden.[6]

In this way, God reassured Perpetua and steeled her spirit for the combat ahead. Even though her persecutors would murder her, if she remained faithful, she would be victorious and ascend to heaven. Like the Blessed Virgin Mary before her, through her faith and obedience, she would crush the head of the Serpent, the ancient Dragon.

Not Against Flesh and Blood

The day before her martyrdom, Perpetua had one last vision. She saw a deacon, who had earlier been executed for his faith, come to the prison and call for her. He was wearing the white robe of the martyr, "richly ornamented." He said to her, "Perpetua, we're waiting for you. Come!"

Then he took her by the hand and led her out of the prison "through rough and winding places" to the arena in the amphitheater where she was to be thrown to the wild

---

[6] *Martyrdom*, I, 3.

beasts. "Don't fear," he told her. "I'm here with you, and I'm laboring with you."

As the dream continued, the mob filled the amphitheater, but Perpetua was puzzled that there were no hungry beasts with her in the arena. Weren't they to be the instruments of her martyrdom?

Then suddenly a tall Egyptian gladiator, "horrible in appearance," entered the arena and prepared himself for combat. Perpetua found herself becoming like one of the male gladiators who was stripped down for the contest by handsome young assistants and rubbed with oil, as was their custom. Then an immense man, the gladiatorial trainer, strode into the arena and offered a green branch with golden apples to whichever combatant won the fight. The contest began.

> We drew near to each other and began to deal out blows. He sought to lay hold of my feet, while I struck at his face with my heels. I was lifted up in the air and began in this way to thrust at him as if I had spurned the earth.
>
> But when I saw that there was some delay in his response, I joined my hands so as to twine my fingers with one another. Then I took hold of his head, and he fell on his face, and I stomped on his head.
>
> The people began to shout, and my assistants to celebrate. I approached the trainer and took the branch; he kissed me and said to me, "Daughter, peace be with you." Then I began my glorious approach to the arena gate.[7]

Perpetua's account of the dream ends with her interpretation of what she saw, with words that echoed the declaration of St. Paul that our spiritual combat is not with flesh and blood, but with the powers of darkness (see Eph 6:12). "Then I awoke," she concluded, "and realized that I was not

---

[7] *Martyrdom*, III, 2.

to fight with beasts, but against the Devil. Still I knew that the victory was awaiting me." [8]

The Impure Spirit Feared Her

At that point, Perpetua's prison diary concluded. But witnesses of the new Christians' martyrdoms a few days later added their testimony to the account. They reported that the brave men and women entered the arena joyfully. Perpetua sang psalms to God, "already treading underfoot the head" of the Dragon.

When they passed by the procurator, they warned him solemnly: "You judge us, but God will judge you."

At the insistence of the mob, they were flogged before each one was exposed to the beasts. When her turn came, Perpetua was gored and thrown by a wild cow. She stood up and rearranged her disheveled hair, noting that she didn't want to look like she was mourning when she actually was in her glory. One by one, the others were attacked by various beasts as well.

The last words of this courageous spiritual gladiator were spoken to her dying comrades: "Stand fast in the faith, and love one another, all of you, and don't allow my sufferings to cause you to stumble." Then the mortally wounded warriors gathered themselves together in the arena and gave one another the kiss of peace.

At last, each one was dispatched by a gladiator with the thrust of a sword. Perpetua was pierced between the ribs and cried out, but then she herself guided to her throat the wavering right hand of the youthful gladiator assigned to kill her. Only then did she die.

One of the Christians of Carthage later speculated about why she would need to assist her executioner. "Perhaps," he observed, "such a woman could not have been slain unless she herself had willed it, because the impure spirit feared her." [9]

---

[8] *Martyrdom*, III, 2.
[9] *Martyrdom*, IV, 4.

- CHAPTER 6 -

ST. ANTHONY OF THE DESERT
Spearhead of an Invasion Force
(c. 251–356)

*The Spirit immediately drove Him out into the wilderness.
And He was in the wilderness forty days, tempted by
Satan; and He was with the wild beasts.*
Mark 1:12–13

Around the year 251, a child was born to wealthy land-owner parents in a town of Lower Egypt, and they called him Anthony. The imperial persecutions had continued in waves for almost two centuries, but for the time being, Egypt was a relatively safe place for a Christian boy to grow up. When his parents died, he disposed of his inheritance, arranged for his sister to be cared for, and set up a small hermitage in the desert land not far from town.

Our Lord had engaged and overcome Satan in combat out in the wilderness. Anthony's mission was to imitate His engagement and His victory and to teach others to do the same. They would become the pioneers of monastic life.

The Devil's First Assault

The story of Anthony's struggles are best told by St. Athanasius, bishop of the great Egyptian city of Alexandria. Athanasius admired the fortitude of the desert hermit, in part because the bishop himself was a great spiritual champion.

The Enemy's strategy against their generation included not only worldly temptations but also heretical movements that denied the truths of the Gospel and divided the Church. God had called Athanasius to oppose those movements, and though his efforts eventually bore fruit, the bishop suffered miserably at the hands of his opponents.

What kinds of battles did Anthony fight and win? The following accounts from Athanasius tell about Anthony's struggles and victory.[1]

*   *   *   *

The Devil, who hates and envies what is good, could not endure to see such resolve in a youth. So he set to work to carry out against Anthony the kinds of things he usually does. First, he tried to lead him away from the discipline of his new way of life.

He whispered to him about his former wealth, care for his sister, the bonds of kinship, love of money, love of glory, the many pleasures of the table, and the other kinds of leisure in life. He reminded the youth as well of the difficulty of virtue and the labor necessary to develop it because of bodily weakness and the patience required. In a word, Satan raised in Anthony's mind a great dust cloud of debate, wishing to prevent him from his fixed purpose.

But the Enemy saw himself to be too weak for Anthony's determination. He himself was actually conquered by the youth's firmness, overcome by his great faith, and thrown for a fall through his constant prayers. So finally the Devil put his trust in "the weapons that hang at his waist" (see

---

[1] These accounts are drawn from St. Athanasius, *Life of Anthony*, trans. H. Ellershaw, in Philip Schaff and Henry Wace, eds., *A Select Library of the Nicene and Post-Nicene Fathers of the Christian Church*, second series (repr., Grand Rapids, Mich.: William B. Eerdmans, 1987), vol. IV, *Select Writings and Letters of Athanasius, Bishop of Alexandria*, 188–221, par. 5–11.

Jb 40:11), boasting in them, for they are his first snare for the young.

He attacked the young man, disturbing him by night and harassing him by day, so that even onlookers saw the struggle that was going on between them. The one would suggest foul thoughts, and the other would counter them with prayers. The former would fire him with lust, but the other, blushing in modesty, would fortify his body with faith, prayers, and fasting.

One night the Devil, that miserable creature, even took on the appearance of a woman and imitated all her gestures, simply to beguile Anthony. But the youth—filling his thoughts with Christ, the nobility inspired by Him, and the dignity of the soul—quenched the coal of the other's deceit.

Again the Enemy reminded him of the delights of pleasure. But Anthony, angered and grieved, focused his thoughts on the threatened fire and gnawing worm of hell (see Mk 9:48). Utilizing these thoughts as weapons against his adversary, he passed through the temptation unscathed.

All this was a source of shame to Anthony's foe. For he, thinking himself like God, was now mocked by a young man, and the one who gloried over flesh and blood was being put to flight by a man in the flesh. For the Lord was working with Anthony—the Lord who for our sake took flesh and gave the body victory over the Devil, so that all who truly fight can say, "Not I, but the grace of God which is with me" (1 Cor 15:10). . . .

A Second Battle

Although the Evil One had fallen, Anthony did not grow careless—nor did the Enemy, finally conquered, cease to lay snares for him. For again he went around like a lion seeking some occasion against him (see 1 Pt 5:8).

But Anthony, having learned from the Scriptures that the strategies of the Devil are many, zealously continued his bodily discipline, concluding that though the Devil had not been able to deceive his heart by bodily pleasure, he would try to ensnare him by other means, for the Demon loves sin. . . . So Anthony decided to practice a stricter discipline. . . .

Mastering himself in this way, Anthony went out to the tombs, which happened to be at a distance from the village, to meditate and pray. He was invading the Enemy's own turf, for the demons often haunted that place. Anthony asked one of his acquaintances to shut him in and bring him bread from time to time. Once he had entered one of the tombs, the other man shut the door on him, so that he remained inside alone.

But the Enemy could stand it no longer, for he feared that in a short time, Anthony would fill the desert with monks who came to imitate his way of life. So the Devil showed up one night with a mob of demons. He whipped Anthony with such force that the hermit lay on the ground speechless from the terrible pain. Anthony later insisted that the torture had been so excessive that no blows inflicted by men could ever have caused him such torment.

By the providence of God—for the Lord never overlooks those who hope in Him—the very next day, Anthony's acquaintance came to bring him bread. When he opened the door and saw Anthony lying on the ground as though dead, he lifted him up and carried him to the church in the village, laying him upon the ground. And many of his relatives and the villagers sat around him as if they were mourning his death.

Around midnight, however, Anthony regained consciousness and stood up. When he saw them all asleep, with his comrade alone keeping watch, he motioned with his head for his comrade to approach and asked him to carry him back to the tomb without waking anyone. So Anthony was carried there by the man, who closed the door to the tomb, leaving Anthony alone.

Anthony could not stand up because of his wounds, but he prayed as he lay there. And after he had prayed, he shouted out, "Here am I—Anthony! I do not run away from your lashes, for even if you inflict more on me, nothing shall separate me from the love of Christ!" (see Rom 8:35). And then he sang the words of the psalm, "Though a host encamp against me, my heart shall not fear!" (Ps 27:3).

Anthony Wins Again

Such were the thoughts and words of this monk. But the Enemy, who hates good, marveled that after the blows, Anthony had dared to return. So he called together his hounds and shouted, exploding with rage, "You see that we failed to stop this man by the spirit of lust or by lashes. Instead, he challenges us. We must attack him in another way."

Changes in appearance are easy for the Devil. So that night, Satan made such a din that the whole place seemed to be shaken by an earthquake. The demons, as if breaking through the four walls of the room and entering through them, appeared in the forms of beasts and creeping things. The place was at once filled with the forms of lions, bears, leopards, bulls, serpents, asps, scorpions, and wolves.

Each of them was moving according to its form. The lion was roaring, ready to attack; the bull seemed to thrust with its horns; the serpent was slithering but unable to approach; and the wolf rushed right toward him. Altogether, the noises of the apparitions, with their angry raging, were dreadful.

Anthony, struck and goaded by them, felt bodily pains still worse. He lay there alert in spirit, however, with an unshaken soul, even as he groaned from bodily anguish. His mind was clear, and he mocked the demons this way: "If there had been any power in you, it would have been enough for just one of you to come. But since the Lord has made you weak, you attempt to terrify me by your numbers. And a further proof of your weakness is that you take the shapes of brute beasts."

Again, with boldness, he said, "If you are able and have received power against me, don't delay to attack. But if you are unable, why trouble me in vain? For faith in our Lord is a seal and a wall of safety to us." So after many attempts, they gnashed their teeth because of him, because they had made fools of themselves rather than him.

In all this, the Lord did not forget Anthony's wrestling but was at hand to help him. Looking up, the monk saw the roof opened, as it seemed, and a ray of light descending on him. The demons suddenly vanished, the pain of his body immediately ceased, and the building was again intact.

Seeing that help had come, getting his breath again, and being freed from pain, Anthony addressed the vision that had appeared to him, saying, "Where were You? Why didn't You appear at the beginning to stop my pains?"

A voice replied, "Anthony, I was here, but I waited to watch your struggle. Since you have endured and have not been defeated, I will always be your Helper, and I will make your name known everywhere." Having heard this, Anthony arose and prayed and received such strength that he felt his body had more power than before.

The Silver Dish

The next day . . . Anthony set off for the mountain to live there. The Enemy saw his zeal and wanted to thwart it, so he cast in his path what seemed to be a great silver dish. He hoped the monk would covet it or even steal it. But Anthony, recognizing the wiles of the Evil One, stood looking at the dish and exposed the Devil's hand in it.

He said, "How does a dish come to lie here in the desert? This road is not well traveled, nor is there here any trace of a wanderer. It could not have fallen without being missed, on account of its size. And anyone who had lost it and turned back to look for it would have found it, for this is a desert place. This is some wile of the Devil.

"You Evil One, you won't turn me from my purpose with this! May it perish with you!" And when Anthony said this, it vanished like smoke from a fire.

ᵥ ᵥ ʌ ʌ

Exorcisms

After nearly twenty years of solitary life, the time came for Anthony to emerge from his mountain hermitage and minister to those in need. His fame grew—just as God had promised—and people came from near and far to ask for his help. Many approached him to seek exorcism for those possessed by demons, and the Lord showed His power through him again and again.

Once he had retired for the night and was determined that he would spend some time without leaving his cell or allowing anyone else to enter. But a military captain named Martianus came to his door seeking help for his demon-possessed daughter. Anthony did not answer the door. But the captain refused to leave, just like the persistent man who came knocking on a friend's door late at night in Our Lord's parable (see Lk 11:5-8).

After Martianus kept beating on the door and calling out to the monk to come and pray for the child, Anthony finally replied. But he spoke without opening the door.

"Man, why do you cry out to me?" he asked the captain. "I too am a man like you. But if you believe in Christ, whom I serve, go home, and according to your faith, pray to God, and it will be done."

Martianus immediately left, believing and calling on Christ. His daughter was then cleansed of the demon.[2]

On another occasion, some esteemed pagan philosophers came to Anthony to argue with him about his faith

---

[2] *Life of Anthony*, 209, par. 48.

in Christ. Though he lacked formal education, he stood his own in the debate. But when it went on without resolution, he finally concluded with a challenge.

Several demon-possessed men had been brought to him for a cure. So Anthony called them over and said to the philosophers, "Look! Here are some who are tormented by demons. Can you cleanse them either by arguments or by whatever art or magic you choose, calling upon your pagan idols? If not, lay aside your argument with us, and you shall see the power of the Cross of Christ."

Then he called on Christ and made the Sign of the Cross several times on those who were suffering. Immediately the men stood up, cured and in their right mind. The philosophers were amazed.

Anthony said to them, "Why do you marvel at this? We aren't the ones who do these things, but it is Christ who does them by means of those who believe in Him. So believe, you yourselves, as well, and you will see that what we have is not skill with words, but faith through love that works in us for Christ. If you yourselves obtain it, you will no longer seek proofs through arguments but will consider faith in Christ sufficient."

They marveled at his words, embraced him, and departed, acknowledging that they had benefited from this unlearned man.[3]

"The Desert Is Filled With Monks!"

Anthony once gave an extended series of instructions to the other monks about who the Devil is and how we must resist him. His words were filled with practical insights about how to deal with temptation and how to respond when the Enemy attacks through more extraordinary phenomena, just like those he himself had endured.

---

[3] *Life of Anthony*, 217, par. 80.

He recalled at that time an episode in which Satan appeared to him, lamenting the holy labors of the monks, which he had been unable to stop. Once the wilderness had been his territory, the place where his demons haunted the tombs and incited evil men to lawless deeds. But with the coming of Anthony, all that had changed.

"I no longer have a place!" the Devil shouted. "No weapon, no city. There are Christians everywhere. And even the desert has filled with monks!" [4]

Why had so many Christian men and women come to follow Anthony's path into the monastic life?

In the year 313, the Emperor Constantine had issued the Edict of Milan. It had granted Christians religious liberty and mandated that the properties confiscated from them be restored. The Church was finally at peace with the Empire.

But she could never be at peace with her ancient Enemy. When the imperial government no longer provided him a bludgeon to beat her, he turned his attention to more subtle strategies. In the great cities of the Empire especially, he wove intricate webs of temptation sure to snare his unsuspecting prey. Those who lusted for power, wealth, fame, or pleasure found ample opportunity to indulge their passions and lose their souls.

Anthony had been among the first to recognize the dangers. Even before the persecutions had ended, he had concluded that combat with the Devil could rage just as fiercely in times of prosperity as in times of persecution. His illustrious example blazed a trail for countless Christian men and women to flee the temptations and distractions of the cities and towns to live a life in the wilderness more focused on God.

The Devil's complaint about the monks thus serves as a fine summary of what Anthony accomplished in his lifelong spiritual battle, which lasted more than a century. In

---

[4] *Life of Anthony*, 207, par. 40–41.

essence, he was the spearhead of an invasion force. Through his courage, his humility, and his discipline, this holy man recaptured considerable enemy territory—not just in the wilderness but in countless souls—and extended the boundaries of the kingdom of light.

- CHAPTER 7 -

ST. BENEDICT OF NURSIA
Conquering With the Sign of the Cross
(c. 480–547)

*But [Jesus] turned to Peter and said, "Get behind
me, Satan! You are a hindrance to me."*
Matthew 16:23

The monastic movement of which Anthony was a forerunner first flourished in the dry, rocky deserts of the
Middle East and North Africa. But that remarkable mode
of spiritual combat eventually made its way to the green,
wooded wilderness of western Europe as well. And it arrived
none too soon.

By the late fifth century, much of the Roman Empire
in the east had remained stable and prosperous. But in the
west, the Empire was collapsing under the weight of Roman
weakness and decadence—hastened by the invasion of tribal
peoples from the wilds of northern and eastern Europe. In
the year 410, Rome had been sacked by invading Visigoths,
and many of her citizens were killed or captured. Then, in
476, the emperor himself was deposed by a tribal chieftain
who was serving as a mercenary in the Roman army.

In Rome and throughout the West, chaos and conflict
ruled the day. The ancient Enemy of our race was no doubt
pleased.

Soon after the last emperor had been removed, however, a child was born into the midst of this political and cultural decay. He was destined to shine a great light into the gathering darkness, and his name was Benedict, "the blessed one."

Benedict was born around the year 480 in Nursia, a city in southern Italy. He was descended from a noble Roman family that had included imperial senators and generals. When it was time for him to be educated, his parents sent him to Rome for his studies.

Benedict, the Hermit

The notorious vices of that great city scandalized Benedict. While countless other young men succumbed to the Enemy's temptations, the holiness of this youth served as armor against such assaults. Around the year 500, he resolved to live a quieter, more solitary life, so he moved to the little town of Enfide, thirty miles away.[1]

Yet even there he failed to find the way of life he desired, so he left and went out into the wilderness, to a remote place called Subiaco. On the way, he met a hermit named Romanus, who gave him a habit and helped him learn the solitary life. Benedict settled in a cave, unknown to anyone except Romanus, and the older monk Romanus shared his bread with the younger Benedict.

Access to the cave was so difficult that Romanus had to tie a loaf to a long cord and let it down to Benedict. It had a little bell tied to it, whose tinkling would alert the

---

[1] This account of Benedict's spiritual battles is drawn largely from the biography written by Pope St. Gregory the Great, found in book IV of his *Dialogues*, written around the year 593. Gregory was the first Benedictine pope, born a few years before Benedict's death, and he based his account on first-person testimony from several of the saint's close associates. The dialogue here is adapted from *The Life of St. Benedict, Patriarch of the Western Monks*, in Edward van Speybrouck, *Father Paul of Moll, 1824–1896: Benedictine Wonder-Worker* (repr., Rockford, Ill.: TAN Books, 1979), 289–332. That version is taken from a 1638 English translation of the work.

young monk that the gift was descending. But according to Benedict's later recollection, already the Devil was growing hostile to the young man's vocation.

Hating both the younger man's life of prayer and the older man's generous charity, the Demon one day threw a stone to break the bell. Despite that minor annoyance, Romanus continued to assist Benedict the best he could. But it was a small foreshadowing of what was to come.

Temptation of the Flesh

Within three years, despite his wish to be solitary, Benedict's life of holy discipline became widely known in the area. People came to bring him food and to receive prayer and counsel.

One day when the holy man was alone, the Tempter tried to harass him. A small black thrush began to fly around his face, so close that he could have reached out and grabbed the bird. But apparently it was not a bird at all. For as soon as Benedict made the Sign of the Cross, it vanished.

Soon after, the young monk was assailed by a sexual temptation that was stronger than any he had ever felt before. The evil spirit brought to his imagination the vivid memory of an attractive woman he had once seen. The image inflamed his heart powerfully with burning lust.

Almost overcome by the passion, Benedict was so discouraged that he began thinking he should leave the wilderness and return to his old way of life. But God's grace came to his assistance, and he suddenly came to himself again.

The monk now saw nearby a thicket full of nettles and briars, so he stripped off his habit and threw himself naked into the middle of those sharp, stinging thorns. He rolled around in them so long that when he finally stopped and stood up, his body was scratched all over.

His first biographer, Pope St. Gregory the Great, reported the consequences of this severe self-discipline: "By the wounds of his flesh, he cured those of his soul. And after that time, as he himself related to his disciples, he was so free from similar temptations that he never felt such passion again." [2]

Soon after, young men began to abandon the world to place themselves under his rule. Freed from vice, he became a teacher of virtue.

The Poisoned Drink

The Enemy soon decided to take a different strategy to ruin Benedict. When the abbot in a nearby monastery died, his monks came to Benedict and sought earnestly to persuade him to become their new leader. For a long time he refused them, warning that his way of life was stricter than theirs. But finally they overcame his caution by their persistent pleading, and he became their abbot.

As it turned out, Benedict's concerns were well grounded. His discipline seemed to the other monks too severe, and in time, they became resentful. Eventually, resentment gave way to bitter rage, and at the Enemy's provocation, they plotted to kill him.

Benedict's wine was poisoned. The monks brought the wine glass to him first to receive the abbot's blessing, as was their custom. But when he stretched out his hand and made the Sign of the Cross over the glass, it shattered, as if he had cast a stone at it.

The abbot knew immediately what had happened. As St. Gregory observed, "The drink of death could not endure the sign of life." Benedict stood up, and his face showed no sign of anger, because his mind was at peace.

Calling the monks together, he addressed them. "May Almighty God forgive you, brothers. Why have you dealt with me in this way? Didn't I warn you that my way of life

---

[2] Van Speybrouck, 302-3.

and yours wouldn't agree? Go and find a superior to your liking, for you can no longer have me with you." Then he left them and returned to his previous way of life.[3]

Once again, the Enemy's plans had been thwarted. Now men from many places came to join Benedict, and soon he had established twelve monasteries, each with twelve monks and a superior.

The Demonic Idol

One day the abbot came to a castle called Cassino, situated on the side of a tall mountain. There stood a temple where the old pagan god Apollo was still worshipped by some people who lived nearby. All around it grew groves where idolatrous sacrifices were offered and the god's alleged sexual conquests of both men and women were celebrated.

Centuries before, St. Paul had warned, "What pagans sacrifice, they offer to demons, and not to God. I do not want you to be partners with demons" (1 Cor 10:20; see also Dt 32:17). Recognizing the diabolical nature of the site, Benedict went to work.

He broke down the idol of Apollo there, turned over the altar, and burned the groves. Then he turned the temple into chapels for St. Martin and St. John. Finally, he preached the gospel to the people, and many were converted to the Christian faith.

But the Enemy was furious with this development. He appeared to Benedict, all on fire with flaming mouth and flashing eyes, raging against him. The other monks could hear his screams but could not see him.

"Benedict! Benedict!" he shouted. But the monk refused to reply. Finally the wicked fiend mocked him: "Not Benedict, but Maledict!"—that is, not the blessed one, but the one

---

[3] Van Speybrouck, 302–4.

accursed. "What have you to do with me, and why do you persecute me?"

Then the abbot considered it advisable for them to exca-vate the place where he had seen the demon stand. When they had dug down to a good depth, they found a bronze idol. For the time being, they disposed of it in the garbage of the monastery kitchen.

While Benedict was busy elsewhere, suddenly there appeared to be a flame rising up from the idol. It looked to the monks as if the whole kitchen were on fire. So they began throwing buckets of water to put out the flames.

Hearing the ruckus, the abbot came to the kitchen and could see no fire. Then he knew it was a demonic apparition intended to confuse and deceive the monks. So he bowed his head in prayer and instructed them to make the Sign of the Cross over their eyes. When they did, they could no longer see the counterfeit blaze.[4]

The Immoveable Stone

One day as the brothers were building the cells of the clois-ter, they found a stone that was well suited to be included in the building. When several men found that they couldn't lift it, they called for the others. But all of them together failed to lift the stone; no matter how hard they labored, it was immoveable.

The monks concluded that the Devil himself was obstructing their work by holding it fast to the earth. So they called for the abbot to come help them by his prayers to drive away the Enemy.

When Benedict arrived, he prayed and then blessed the stone. Immediately, they were able to lift it as if it had scarcely any weight at all. The construction of the cloister continued.

---

[4] Van Speybrouck, 310–11.

Exorcism of a Cleric

In the church of Aquino, a small town not far from Cassino, one of the clerics who had received the tonsure but had not yet received holy orders as a priest was tormented by an evil spirit. The bishop of that diocese, Constantius, had sent him to various martyrs' shrines to be cured. But apparently the martyrs refrained from healing him so that God's gifts of grace in Benedict might be made manifest to everyone.

Finally, the cleric was brought to Benedict. When the abbot prayed to Jesus Christ for the man, the unclean spirit was driven out. But the holy man knew the cleric's heart, and he warned him with this command: "Go, and after this, eat no meat, and don't presume to receive holy orders. For on the day you receive holy orders, you will again become slave to the Devil."

So the clerk went on his way, healed. For a while, Benedict's warning made a strong impression on him, and he obeyed his command. But after many years, he began to envy those who had received holy orders. So he finally laid aside the abbot's words and received them himself.

Right away, the same demon who had possessed him took power over him again. The unclean spirit never stopped tormenting him until the day he died.[5]

The Devil on a Mule

One day Benedict was going to St. John's oratory, which stands on the top of a mountain. On the way, he met what appeared to be a man riding a mule, in the clothes of a physician and carrying a physician's instruments. When Benedict asked him where he was going, he said he was going to administer a potion.

The abbot went on to the chapel to pray. But when he finished praying, he realized that something was wrong,

---

[5] Van Speybrouck, 317–18.

so he hurried back to the monastery. The "physician," it turned out, had actually been a demon, and when he had found one of the senior monks drawing water, he entered him immediately.

The demon threw the unfortunate man to the ground and tortured him mercilessly. But as soon as Benedict returned and found the monk cruelly tormented, the holy man slapped him on the cheek, driving out the wicked spirit. It never dared to return again.

The Monk and the Dragon

One of Benedict's monks was continually wavering in his commitment to the monastic way of life. He would frequently beg to be released, but Benedict would always urge him to be constant in his resolve. Nevertheless, the monk persisted, so the abbot finally consented and told him to leave the community.

He was only a short distance from the monastery when he met a dragon on the road, coming toward him with his mouth open to swallow him alive. Terrified, the monk began to quake, crying out, "Help! Help! This dragon will devour me!"

Hearing his cries, the brothers ran out to where he stood. But they could see no dragon. So they took the monk, panting with fright, back again to the monastery.

Safely within the cloister, the monk promised never to leave again. From that time onward, he remained faithful to his promise. As it turns out, Benedict had prayed for his eyes to be opened so that he could see that the Devil was ready to devour him. That way he could know for certain that the monastic way of life was his safeguard against the Enemy.[6]

---

[6] Van Speybrouck, 330.

The St. Benedict Medal

All these instances from the life of St. Benedict demonstrate his remarkable prowess as a spiritual warrior. Having learned to resist effectively the temptations of the Enemy, he received the graces of a remarkable wisdom to discern the activity of unclean spirits and an abiding authority to command and banish them.

By the time he went on to his reward in the year 547, Benedict's reputation was widely and firmly established. Miracles were often worked through his intercession. Of particular import was the miraculous healing of an eleventh-century youth named Bruno, who had been bitten by a venomous snake and was near death.

When all hope of Bruno's recovery had been lost, he had a vision of a radiant ladder that reached to heaven. Descending the ladder was St. Benedict, holding a luminous cross, which he touched to Bruno's face. The young man was instantly healed and the vision ended.

Bruno later entered the Benedictine order and went on to become pope in 1048, taking the name Leo IX. He enriched with special blessings a medal bearing the image of the holy abbot on one side and a cross on the other, and its use spread throughout the Church. In 1742, Pope Benedict XIV solemnized use of the medal and recommended it to the faithful.

This St. Benedict medal has come to be known as the "devil-chasing medal." It typically has on its reverse side the initial letters of the Latin words in an ancient prayer against the Evil One, which begins, *Vade retro satana* ("Get back, Satan!"). The command is reminiscent of Jesus' exclamation, "Get behind me, Satan!" (see Mt 16:23).

The rest of the prayer says, "Never tempt me with your vanities! What you offer me is evil. Drink the poison yourself!" Down through the ages, those who know the story about how the abbot was protected from drinking poison find in those words a great consolation that the Enemy has been decisively defeated.

- CHAPTER 8 -

ST. MEINRAD
Assisted by an Angel
(c. 797–861)

Then the Devil left Him, and behold,
angels came and ministered to Him.
Matthew 4:11

And when the Devil had ended every temptation,
he departed from Him until an opportune time.
Luke 4:13

The centuries in western Europe immediately following St. Benedict's life have been dubbed the Dark Ages. The name can in many ways be justified. After the central Roman authority was lost, political instability and military conflict were widespread. An entire way of life had passed away.

The barbarian invaders, now settlers, were largely unacquainted with intellectual pursuits such as literature, philosophy, jurisprudence, and technology. Cultural decline resulted. Classical literature was lost, illiteracy became the norm, and legal standards were compromised.

The once-vibrant economy of the Empire went into decline; cities and towns began to shrink. Buildings, roads, and aqueducts were no longer well maintained. Land and sea routes were infested with highway robbers and pirates, strangling commerce. Crime increased, and brutal barbarian tribal law prevailed. Fear and uncertainty about the future were pervasive.

The Prince of Darkness was no doubt pleased. But he hadn't counted on heaven's emerging strategy to oppose his kingdom: New Benedictine monasteries were springing up across the continent like stars in the midnight sky.

These communities became seeds of spiritual life and civilized culture. They evangelized the barbarian peoples and became the chief centers of learning, serving as seminaries for priests and bishops and teaching people to read. Laboriously copying manuscripts of classical works of literature and learning, the monks preserved the ancient wisdom.

It was also the monks who cleared new areas in the forests and swamps and extended the domain of agriculture. They developed new technologies not just for agriculture but also for stonework, carpentry, ironwork, food processing, and more. Then they taught these skills to the people around them.

A Benedictine Priest

Toward the end of the eighth century, while a small renaissance of civility was at last appearing among the Franks under Charlemagne, there was born in that region known as Swabia a child named Meinrad. He was destined, as a spiritual son of Benedict, to help bring the light of God to that part of the world.[1]

---

[1] This account is based on two biographical sketches of Meinrad. One is "S. Meinrad, H.M.," found in Sabine Baring-Gould, *The Lives of the Saints* (London: John Hodges, 1877), vol. 1, 321–30. The other was written in Latin, probably in the tenth century, by a monk in the Abbey of Reichenau. The text is found in the *Vita S. Meginrati*, ed. O. Holder-Egger, *Monumenta Germaniae Historica, Scriptores*, vol. 15, pt. 1, 444–48. Direct quotes are drawn from an English translation of this text, *The Life of Venerable Meinrad the Hermit*, by the monks of St. Meinrad Archabbey in Indiana, which was accessed on July 13, 2015, at http://www.saintmeinrad.edu/the-monastery/life-of-st-meinrad/.

Meinrad was educated in the Benedictine abbey school at Reichenau, an island on Lake Constance in what is now Switzerland, where one of his kinsmen was abbot. He became a priest and entered the abbey there. Soon after, he was sent to serve as master of a school at a small priory in the remote wilderness at the upper end of Lake Zurich.

The young monk's wisdom, modesty, and learning earned him the favor of all those who knew him. But Meinrad had been reading about the great hermits of the ancient deserts. Though his life as a teacher bore rich fruit, he longed for solitude, where he could practice prayer and meditation without distraction.

After scouting the wilderness, the monk finally found a remote place in the dense forest on Mount Etzel in the Swiss Alps, where he could he could live the life of a contemplative. At his request, his superior sadly granted him permission to go. Meinrad departed, taking with him nothing but his Missal, *The Rule of St. Benedict*, and a few other books. He was thirty-one years old.

The holy man established a hermitage there on the secluded mountainside. He lived in a small hut of pine logs, with a crude chapel alongside. A widow living in a village not too far away brought him humble but regular provisions.

For seven years, Meinrad lived there, strengthening his spiritual armor by frequent prayer and fasting and receiving the powerful graces of the Blessed Sacrament as he celebrated Mass. The fame of his holiness spread, however, and like his predecessor Benedict, he attracted a multitude of visitors. They flocked to him for counsel, for comfort, and for prayer. His radiant presence was causing the darkness to retreat all around him.

Combat in the Wilderness

Eventually the monk decided to move farther into the wilderness so that he could regain his solitude. He found a place even more remote in the vast forest, where he built another log hut near a spring. The abbess of a convent at Zurich sent food and other provisions occasionally, but at least for the time being, he was alone again at last.

Or so he thought. For even though Meinrad had found a place far from other human beings, his cell was known to the Enemy of his soul, who resented the good he had done for so many people. So the monk moved into a new realm of spiritual combat. As an early biographer from the abbey at Reichenau observed, "From battle in common with his brothers, he entered into the single contest of the desert." That biographer went on to describe the conflict:

> One day while he was praying, it happened that a great host of demons surrounded him from every side, and the servants of darkness so overshadowed him that he could no longer see even the light of day. With terrible threats and the greatest dread, they exhausted him. Prostrate in prayer, as the situation then required, he commended himself with every desire to the holy Lord. Things went on in this way for a long time.

But Meinrad was not alone with his adversaries. Soon heaven sent an angelic warrior to his aid:

> Then, he saw a light from the east. Following this light, an angel came to him where he was lying prostrate in prayer in the midst of the evil spirits; and with great authority, the angel ordered the impious array to depart and to dare not inflict further temptation or terror on Meinrad. After the host left, the angel consoled Meinrad, as one friend another, and departed.

Though the conflict had been fierce, it resulted in a major victory for the holy monk. The account concludes, "And so from that day on . . . he suffered no further terror from evil spirits." [2]

---

[2] *Monumenta*, at the web page cited.

In this experience, the monk was imitating his Lord, who in the wilderness had been strengthened by an angel after the Devil departed (see Mt 4:11). But also like his Lord, Meinrad would find that the Enemy was withdrawing "until an opportune time" to return (Lk 4.13).

The Final Assault

For twenty-six years, the holy man remained in that remote spot, fasting and praying and focusing on God in contemplation. At times he had thoughts of leaving the rigors of solitude in such a wild place, especially on nights when he shivered in the bitter cold. But he viewed such thoughts as temptations from the Enemy, and he always found the grace to resist them by intensifying his prayer and fasting.

Once day a carpenter, searching the forest for wood, came across his hut. Soon afterward, hunters came visiting, and before long, a stream of pilgrims followed, seeking his prayers, counsel, and blessing. He found himself in much the same situation as he had faced at Mount Etzel.

The flow of visitors became more like a flood when the new abbess of the convent at Zurich gave him a statue of the Madonna and Child. Pilgrims soon came to venerate the image, and they left behind gifts. Meinrad kept those presents that could adorn the chapel. The others he gave away to the poor.

At last the day came when the Devil sent his agents—human ones this time—for a final assault on his life. Two evil men concluded that the monk must have a hidden cache of treasure collected from the pilgrims. They resolved to have it for their own.[3]

---

[3] This final anecdote of the saint's martyrdom comes primarily from Baring-Gould, 329-30.

And so "it came about," says his early biographer, "by the inspiration of the one who entered the serpent and through its mouth deceived our first parents and threw them out of paradise, that [the] two men made their way to his cell in order to kill him . . . driven by the terrible spirit with which they were filled." [4]

Nevertheless, God's providence was permitting them to carry out their plan. He had already revealed to Meinrad what was about to happen so that he could prepare himself. The monk celebrated Mass so that he could receive the Eucharist as his viaticum before death.

His Last Fragrant Breath

When the bandits finally discovered the hermitage and approached the chapel door, Meinrad had just concluded the Sacrifice of the Mass. Two ravens, who had been Meinrad's companions since they were fledglings, screamed and fluttered as if to warn the monk. But he lingered a little longer in prayer, then took up the relics of the saints in the chapel and kissed them reverently one by one. He commended his coming passion to them and to the Lord.

When at last Meinrad opened the door, he received them cheerfully. "My friends," he greeted them, "if you had arrived a little earlier, you might have assisted at the Sacrifice. Enter and pray God and His saints to bless you; then come with me and I will give you such refreshments as my poor cell affords."

He left them in the chapel and went to his hut to prepare the meal. But the assassins rushed after him. "I know your intention," he said, smiling. "When I am dead, place one of these tapers at my head, and the other at my feet, and escape as quickly as you can, so as not to be overtaken." [5]

---

[4] *Monumenta*, at the web page cited.
[5] Baring-Gould, 329.

He gave to one robber his tunic and to the other his cloak, along with bread and wine. But one assassin seized and held the monk while the other clubbed him. Without resisting, the holy man raised his hands in prayer.

Eager to finish the evil deed and driven by Satan, the first one grabbed the club from his accomplice and delivered a terrible blow to the old man's head. The victim sank to the ground, still alive, so they threw themselves on him and strangled him to death. When they did, a sweet fragrance issued forth with his last breath and filled the room.

Through Satan's malice, Meinrad was at last freed to stand face to face with the Savior he had served so faithfully.

The Saint's Legacy

The thieves stripped off the monk's habit, put his body in his bed, put a cloak beneath it, and covered it with a blanket. Perhaps beginning to feel a pang of remorse, they honored his request about the candles. They placed one at his head, then took the other into the chapel to light it from the candle that was burning there.

When they returned, they found the unlit candle now burning. Terrified by this sign, they dared not steal anything consecrated to the service of the altar, so they took some clothing and bed coverings and fled back the way they had come. The ravens, still screeching, followed them, pecking and clawing at their heads.

On their way, the thieves were met by the carpenter who had discovered the monk's cell and now recognized the ravens. After entering the chapel and finding the saint murdered, he summoned his family to take care of the body while he apprehended the murderers. Their hiding place was revealed by the ravens who continued to scream at them. The assassins confessed their crimes and were sentenced to death.

Some forty years later, a Swabian priest from a noble family took up residence in Meinrad's deserted hermitage. Though he later was consecrated as Archbishop of Metz, he eventually returned to the hermitage and gathered with him a number of monks. They formed there a Benedictine abbey that has survived times of great tribulation for the Church over the centuries. To this day, it continues the luminous ministry of St. Meinrad, no doubt to the dismay of the Prince of Darkness.[6]

---

[6] Alban Butler, *Butler's Lives of the Saints: Complete Edition*, ed. S. J. Herbert Thurston and Donald Atwater (New York: P. J. Kenedy, 1963), vol. III, 140.

- CHAPTER 9 -

ST. BERNARD
Clarion of the Battle
(1090–1153)

For if the trumpet gives an uncertain sound,
who shall prepare himself to the battle?
1 Corinthians 14:8 (Douay-Rheims)

By the time of Meinrad's martyrdom in 861, western Europe was entering a time of severe troubles. First were the military invasions that devastated cities, towns, and lands across the continent.

Muslim invaders had occupied the Iberian Peninsula and threatened France. They were gaining control of islands in the Mediterranean and making raids on the Italian peninsula, even sacking the Basilicas of St. Peter and St. Paul in Rome. Viking raiders continued to sweep in from the north, terrorizing the British Isles and France, going so far as to plunder and occupy Paris. The Magyars pressed in from the east, pillaging all the way to Germany, France, and Italy.

Worse yet was the corruption in the Church, especially in Rome. Though Pope St. Nicholas I (reigned 858–67) served with heroic holiness, some of his successors on the throne of St. Peter were either too weak or too wicked to accomplish reforms that the Church desperately needed. Ecclesiastical and political parties vied for control of the papacy to use it as their pawn. Several popes were assassinated; others served only a few days or months.

For just one example of Satan's interference in Church affairs of the time, we need only consider Pope John XII, who became pope sometime between the ages of seventeen and twenty-four. According to his contemporaries, he culti-vated many personal vices, including fornication; sold church offices to support his extravagant lifestyle; consecrated boys as bishops as favors to their wealthy fathers; tortured and exiled dissenting clergy; and pilfered the treasury of the Church.

No wonder, then, that John was reported to have toasted the Devil with a glass of wine and invoked demonic pagan gods, such as Jupiter and Venus, when he was gambling. Per-haps most tellingly, it was said that John never made the Sign of the Cross. He was at last deposed by the Emperor Otto I and replaced with a layman of that ruler's choosing.

Reform of the Monasteries

With such deplorable spiritual conditions, even the Benedic-tine monasteries were unable to escape the Enemy's influences. Wealth and worldliness became common among the monks. They often received income from feudal lords, making them obligated to secular political interests. Some abbots even mar-ried, had children, and bequeathed their titles to their heirs.

Yet the time at last came when God raised up spiritual warriors to combat the Enemy's assault on the Church from within. Among the monastic reformers whose heroic efforts not only cleansed the monasteries but transformed the wider society, none was more valiant than Bernard of Clairvaux.

Born in 1091 in a family castle near Dijon in what is now France, Bernard received a good education but lived a frivolous youth. His ways changed after his mother died, however, and he decided to enter religious life.

His gifts of persuasion were evident even at a young age: He convinced thirty of his friends and relatives (including five of his brothers) to join him. His youngest brother and widowed father followed him later.

Bernard chose Cîteaux, recently founded as the first monastery of the new Cistercian reform, which observed a strict interpretation of the Benedictine rule. In 1115, when he was only twenty-four, he was sent with twelve monks to establish a Cistercian monastery at Langres, with Bernard as the abbot. Despite his strict way of life, he soon had scores of disciples, attracted by his personal holiness.

The new monastery's name was changed to Clairvaux. It was to become the motherhouse of some sixty-eight Cistercian monasteries that were established by its brothers. Bernard became renowned throughout Europe for his holiness and wisdom, and before long, he was being consulted by both popes and secular rulers.

Preaching and Exorcisms

In 1130, Bernard began public preaching across the continent, and his words were confirmed with numerous miracles. Many of these were dramatic healings and exorcisms. One of his more sensational battles with Satan took place in the Italian city of Pavia.[1]

As soon as the holy abbot arrived in the city, the house where he was lodging was filled and surrounded with sick people seeking a cure. Reports of his miracles had spread throughout Italy, so people came from near and far. His prayers, his touch, and sometimes just his presence worked miracles. But, most dramatically, those who were possessed by demons were delivered by his word, recovering their minds and their freedom.

Among these was a woman who was brought to the feet of the saint by her husband. Satan immediately began speaking through her, mocking Bernard and referring contemptuously

---

[1] This anecdote is based on the account in Abbé Theodore Ratisbonne, *St. Bernard of Clairvaux: Oracle of the Twelfth Century, 1091–1153* (repr., Charlotte, N.C.: TAN Books, 2012), 192–94.

to the unclean spirit who possessed the poor woman at his command: "This devourer of roots and cabbages will never send away my little dog!"

The woman continued to blaspheme and insult the abbot as the Enemy attempted through her to annoy him and lower him in the estimation of the people around. Nevertheless, Bernard recognized the demonic strategy and began himself to mock the mocker. His gave instructions that the woman was to be taken to the cathedral in Pavia, which contained the relics of St. Syrus, the patron of the city and its first bishop. The humble abbot wanted to leave the honor of curing her to that saint.

But the Devil was not pleased with that plan. So he continued his abuse, saying dismissively, as if he were speaking of children, "Little Syrus won't send me away, and little Bernard won't either!"

The abbot replied firmly: "It will be neither Syrus nor Bernard who will send you away; it will be the Lord Jesus Christ!" Then he began to pray, asking God to assist in the deliverance of this tormented woman.

Right away, the evil spirit changed his tone and his words. The intriguing conversation that followed provides much to ponder.

"Oh, how gladly would I leave this miserable creature," he said. "If only I could escape from the suffering I endure in this body! But I can't."

When Bernard asked why not, the spirit replied, "Because the great Lord would not allow it yet."

"Who, then, is this great Lord?" asked the abbot.

"It is Jesus of Nazareth."

"So you know the Lord Jesus? Have you seen Him?"

"I have seen Him," the demon affirmed.

"Where did you see Him?"

"I have seen Him in glory."

"So you have been in glory?"

"Yes," the demon replied, "I was in glory."

"And how did you lose it?" the abbot asked.

"We fell in great numbers, with Lucifer."

All these words were spoken through the woman, with a sad tone of voice, and everyone around could hear them distinctly.

Finally, Bernard asked a provocative question. "Wouldn't you like to be restored to that glory and to your original condition of happiness?"

Responding in Latin, with an unusual tone of voice, the demon replied, "*Hoc, inquit, tardatum est,*" which means, "That is deferred."

It was a puzzling remark. The Church affirms that the demons will never be restored to their original happiness. But the Devil, of course, is "a liar and the father of lies" (Jn 8:44). Perhaps it was a desperate play for sympathy.

In any case, the woman was now silent, and the demon no longer spoke through her. But Bernard resumed his prayers for her, and at last, he cast the wicked spirit out of her. She started home, completely healed.

The Demon Returns

The people were amazed and joyful at her deliverance. But the joy was short-lived. As soon as the woman entered her own house in another village, the demon returned and entered her body. Then he tormented her with convulsions more violent than she had ever suffered before.

Her poor husband was filled with grief and confusion. On the one hand, it was agonizing to live with someone possessed by a demon. On the other, he loved her, and abandoning her would be wrong. So he determined that he would return to Pavia and carry his wife with him.

When he returned, however, the saint was no longer in town. The people told him that Bernard had gone on to the city of Cremona. So the husband took her there and found him. Weeping, he told the abbot what had happened.

That evening, moved by the husband's tears, the saint spent the whole night in prayer in a nearby church. The next day he cast the demon out from the woman again. But he was concerned that the unclean spirit might try to return once more.

So Bernard instructed her to hang around her neck a note with these words: "Satan, I command you in the name of our Lord Jesus Christ never to be so bold as to approach this woman again!" After that day, she was completely and permanently delivered, living in peace.

Another Demon in Cremona

According to a monk who later recorded Bernard's miracles, in the same city, a demon-possessed man was infamous for his strange howling. Many people laughed at the unfortunate man, but those who were more serious-minded and charitable felt a deep compassion for him.

Whenever the man wanted to speak, he would begin barking like a dog instead. When he saw Bernard approach, he howled like a ferocious dog being beaten by a stick. But the holy man addressed the demon and cast it out in the name of Jesus Christ.

Bernard invited the cured man to speak. He began thanking God for his deliverance. Then he went to the church, attended Mass, and "continued to fulfill all the duties of a reasonable and grateful man." [2]

The Devil Fell Through Pride

Bernard's consistent attitude toward Satan seems to have been one not of fear but of disdain. In his treatise *On the Steps of Humility and Pride*, he addressed Lucifer directly and reprimanded him:

> You want to set up for yourself a throne in heaven so that you may be like the Most High [Is 14:4].
>
> With what purpose? On what do you rest your confidence? Measure your strength, you fool. . . .

---

[2] Quoted in Ratisbonne, 194.

You deceive yourself, wretch, you deceive yourself, not
God [Ps 26:12]. . . . You are trying to deceive Him, but He
sees everything. You deceive yourself, not God. Despite His
great goodness toward you, you are planning to do Him
wrong, and your wickedness is hateful indeed [35:3]. . . .

O Lucifer, who rose in the morning [Is 14:12], now you are
not light-bearer but bringer of darkness, or even of death.[3]

To the Abbot of Clairvaux, the ancient Enemy was an arrogant, self-deceived pretender to be scorned and dismissed.

The Second Crusade

Yet one more aspect of Bernard's spiritual combat must be noted
because of the prominent role it played in his mission and the
controversy it has stirred up ever since his day: his labors to sum-
mon Christian men to fight the Second Crusade in 1147–48.

No doubt this Crusade was in most regards a disaster.
Not only did it fail to achieve its objectives; it provoked
countless crimes against innocent people who had nothing
to do with those objectives. But we must not blame Bernard's preaching for such failure. Many of those who took
up arms turned out to be immoral men, and more than once
he himself lamented—and tried to stop—their evil deeds.

The abbot's motivations in the matter are clear. In the
first half of the eleventh century, the persecution of Christian
natives and pilgrims had been growing in the Holy Land and
other places that Muslim armies had conquered and occupied.
In 1071, a major defeat of the Byzantine Christian armies in
the Battle of Manzikert made it likely that the great capital
city of Eastern Christendom would itself fall to Muslim forces.
Two thirds of the Christian world had already been conquered
by the armies of Islam. In desperation, the Eastern emperor
asked his Christian brothers in the West for assistance.

---

[3] Bernard of Clairvaux, *Bernard of Clairvaux: Selected Works*, trans. G. R. Evans
(New York: Paulist Press, 1987), 126–27.

The First Crusade had been the response of Western Christians to that call. The Holy Land was recaptured, and several Christian kingdoms were established. But within a generation, the threat of Muslim armies had returned. After they recaptured the city of Edessa, not only Bernard but Pope Eugene III and many other Church and secular leaders as well called for a new crusade.

Those who supported the efforts were convinced that militant Islam would reconquer the Holy Land and threaten the Christians of the Byzantine Empire. In addition, Muslims already occupied most of the Iberian Peninsula, Sicily, Malta, and Crete. They had established strongholds in Italy and were making military excursions into that land and southern France as well. These expansions of Muslim-controlled territory made it a certainty that if the armies of Islam were not defeated, western Europe as well would eventually be conquered and occupied.

For Bernard, then, as for countless others, military warfare against aggressive Muslim forces was at the same time a spiritual warfare against the professed enemies of the Christian faith and the dark powers that were driving them. From Muslim-ruled Syria to Muslim-occupied Spain, those Christians who were most familiar with Muslim beliefs and practices commonly concluded that Muhammad was a "false prophet" misled by demons and a "forerunner of the Antichrist."[4] To oppose the advances of that religion and its oppression of Christians was the duty of every soldier in the service of Christ the King—and Bernard offered a clarion call to that battle.

---

[4] See, for example, the section "On the Heresy of the Ishmaelites" in St. John Damascene, *On Heresies*, vol. 37 of the series *The Fathers of the Church* (Washington, D.C.: Catholic University Press, 1958), 153–60. St. John Damascene (c. 675–749) lived in Syria, a nation that had been largely Christian but had come under Muslim rule. Though the authorship of this particular eighth-century text has been debated, the view of Islam it presents was common among Christians then and in the following centuries.

- CHAPTER 10 -

ST. DOMINIC
Wielding the Word of God
(1170–1221)

Now the Spirit expressly says that in later times
some will depart from the faith by giving heed to
deceitful spirits and doctrines of demons.
1 Timothy 4:1

In the eleventh and twelfth centuries, the ancient Enemy stirred up a new attack on the Church, through the revival of an ancient heresy. It echoed in its teaching and practice the disturbing religion of the old Manicheans, a sect with whom St. Augustine had briefly flirted before his conversion. Known as the Cathari, meaning "the pure ones," the followers of this heresy emerged as a movement in eastern Europe but eventually came to Italy, Germany, and southern France, where they were also called the Albigensians.

The movement brought great disturbance, not only to the Church, but to secular society as well. Though it was characterized by a variety of beliefs and practices, the most common ones threatened civil order. The Cathari claimed that there is not one God but two: One is good and the Creator of the human spirit; the other is evil and the creator of the material world, including the human body. The human spirit is thus imprisoned in the human body by the evil creator, and it must be liberated.

The implications of such views should be clear. The *Perfecti*, those who would be perfect, could not engage in sex, even within marriage, because the body is evil and procreation condemns more spirits to the prison of embodiment. Meat consumption was forbidden because many Cathari also believed that human spirits who weren't perfected at death would be reincarnated as animals. So neither hell nor purgatory existed.

Essential Christian teaching was utterly denied: not just the doctrine of the Blessed Trinity but also of the Incarnation. If the body is evil, then God would never take on human flesh as a Man. Thus Christ had been only a creature who appeared to be a man. His passion, death, and resurrection had all been an illusion, and the bodily resurrection of all the dead was a false hope.

At the same time, the Catholic Church was rejected as evil, not only because it affirmed the ancient apostolic doctrines, but because it offered the sacraments as a means of grace. Each sacrament makes use of some kind of matter: water, bread and wine, oil, bodily actions. So if the material world is evil, then sacraments are worse than useless; they are wicked.

Meanwhile, in place of the sacraments, the Cathari offered a ritual called the *Consulatum*, "the consolation." They claimed it accomplished the forgiveness of all sins, without any attempt at penance, and was a guarantee of entrance into heaven.

Human authority outside their own ranks was largely spurned as illegitimate. The Catholic clergy was reviled, and often secular rulers were as well. The taking of oaths, an act that secured so many aspects of medieval life, was forbidden.

Not surprisingly, both Church and state viewed this movement with increasing alarm. Once the Albigensians in France found political support among some of the nobility, military conflict was inevitable, especially after a papal legate was assassinated. Several nobles and even kings became involved, and after hostilities began, there were atrocities on both sides.

The Albigensians plundered and devastated some towns and regions, and the secular forces allied with the Church—which finally launched a twenty-year crusade against them (1209–29)—were severe in their response. In time, the crusade degenerated into a war of conquest between opposing nobles.[1] The Devil was no doubt immensely pleased.

Preaching as Spiritual Combat

Into the midst of these troubles came St. Dominic, the founder of a new religious order and one of the greatest Catholic preachers of all time. The extent to which he was personally involved in the military actions against the Albigensians is fiercely debated, but one thing is clear: His primary strategy in combat was to speak boldly and compellingly the truth about God, the Church, and the world.[2]

Born in Spain in 1170, Dominic received a university education, entered the Benedictine order, and was ordained. In 1203, he courageously journeyed into the territory where the Albigensians were most numerous to win back their souls. There he was thoroughly reviled and often threatened with death.

The crowds followed him, throwing dirt at him and spitting in his face. He was mocked and insulted, but he accepted the abuse with serenity. His humility was a part of his spiritual armor.

---

[1] A summary of Albigensian teaching and practice, and the resulting conflict in France, can be found in Nicholas Weber, "Albigenses," in *The Catholic Encyclopedia* (New York: Robert Appleton, 1907), vol. 1, 267–69, and J. E. Bresnahan, "Albigenses," in *The New Catholic Encyclopedia* (New York: McGraw-Hill, 1967), vol. 1, 262–63.

[2] For two useful biographies, see Augusta Theodosia Drane, *The Life of Saint Dominic* (repr., Rockford, Ill.: TAN Books, 1988), and Sister Mary Jean Dorcy, O.P., *Saint Dominic* (repr., Rockford, Ill.: TAN Books, 2012). The account here is largely drawn from these two sources.

Once the saint was warned that a party of Albigensians was lying in wait to assassinate him. But the spiritual warrior was undaunted. Instead of avoiding them or trying to slip past them unnoticed, he walked by them in plain sight, cheerfully singing hymns at the top of his voice. Though they stopped him and threatened to kill them, his mild and undisturbed response flabbergasted them, and they let him go his way.

We should note that worldliness was widespread among the clergy of the time, so the strict discipline of the Albigensians offered to many an admirable contrast. But Dominic came preaching barefoot and in a rough habit. His simplicity and poverty disarmed his opponents and helped him win their respect.

Healings and Exorcisms

Several accounts of the friar's missions among the Albigensians reveal the spiritual warfare that raged beneath the surface of events. One night, after a long debate with some of them, Dominic left with a Cistercian monk and went to a nearby church to spend the rest of the night in prayer, as was his custom. But the doors were locked, so they knelt outside and began to pray.

Once they did, however, they suddenly found themselves inside the church before the high altar. They had no idea how they had gotten there. So they continued in prayer until the dawn.

In the morning, the people found them there. Rumors that the holy man could perform miracles had spread through the city, so they gathered at the church, bringing their sick to him to be healed. Among them were several who were possessed by demons.

When Dominic was asked to cast out the demons, he took a stole and placed it around his neck as if he were about to prepare for Mass. But then he removed the stole and placed it around the necks of the possessed. They were immediately delivered.

The Devil Flees

Such miracles enhanced the preacher's reputation among the people and served as signs that the gospel he preached was truly inspired by God. On one occasion, a frightening episode served as a convincing sign that the teaching of the Albigensians was inspired by the Enemy of their souls.

One day as he prayed in the church in the village of Fanjeaux, nine Albigensian women of noble birth came to him in great anguish and threw themselves at his feet. "Servant of God!" they cried out. "If what you preached to us this morning is true, we have till now been living in horrible darkness. Have compassion on us, and teach us how we may be saved!"

Dominic looked on them with a cheerful smile and consoled them with words of hope that God would help them. He prayed for a while, then turned to the women and encouraged them to have courage and not be afraid of what they were about to see.

As soon as he had spoken those words, they saw before them a monstrous beast, ferocious and hideous to behold. It fled from them and appeared to escape through the bell tower of the church. The women were understandably terrified, but Dominic offered them reassurance.

"God has shown you, my daughters," he told them, "how terrible is the Devil whom till now you have served. Thank Him, therefore, for the Evil One has from this moment no more power over you." As a result, the nine women all received instruction in the Catholic faith and were received into a nearby monastery.

The Spread of the Order of Preachers

Dominic's missions among the Albigensians were only a portion of his spiritual combat. In the year 1206, he founded a religious institute for women in their territory, because so many women had succumbed to the heresy. After the formal foundation and papal approval of the Order of Preachers in 1216, he spent the last years of his life dispelling the darkness by traveling across Europe to preach and establish new houses. The new order was astoundingly successful in the conversion of countless souls.

Once again, his preaching was confirmed by numerous miracles, including the exorcism of unclean spirits. Once while in Rome, he preached at the convent attached to the old church of St. Sixtus. It was a community that had been greatly in need of reform, so the Pope had asked him to reform it.

He stood "at the grating"—that is, in the place where his sermon could be heard both by the cloistered nuns and by the congregation that had gathered in the public part of the church. As he preached, a demon-possessed woman interrupted him with shouting.

"You villain!" the demon screamed, using the woman's voice. "These nuns were once all my own, but you have robbed me of them all! But this soul at least is mine, for there are seven of us who have her under our control."

In reply, Dominic commanded the demon to be silent. Then he made the Sign of the Cross. As the entire congregation and all the nuns watched, she was delivered from the tormenting spirits. She left, but a few days later, she returned to him and asked to enter the consecrated life. He consented and placed her in the convent attached to the church where she had been freed from the unclean spirit.

The Devil Pretends to Be a Friar

As at least one biographer has noted, apparently the Evil One was never permitted to do bodily harm to Dominic or assail him with grave temptations. When Satan appeared to him, the Enemy always seemed to be thwarted and despicable, not powerful or seductive. One incident illustrates that reality well:

The servant of God, who had neither bed nor cell of his own, had publicly commanded his children in chapter that in order that they might wake the more promptly to rise to morning prayer, they were to retire to bed at a certain hour, in which he was strictly obeyed.

Now, as he himself remained before the Lord in the church, the Devil appeared before him in the form of one of the brethren. Though it was past the prohibited time, he still remained in the church with an air of special devotion and modesty. So the saint, judging it to be one of the friars, went softly up to him and asked him to go to his cell and sleep with the others.

The pretended friar inclined his head, in a sign of humble obedience, and went as he was bid. But on each of the two following nights, he returned at the same hour and in the same manner. The second time, the man of God rose very gently—although, indeed, he had reason to be somewhat angry, seeing that he had at the table, during the day, reminded everyone to observe the instruction he had given them. Again, he asked him to go away.

He went, but as we have said, he returned yet a third time. Then it seemed to the saint that the disobedience and stubbornness of this brother was too great. So he reproved him for it with some severity.

The Devil desired nothing else but to disturb his prayer and to provoke him to anger—as well as to make him break the rule of silence. So at this, the demon gave a loud laugh and leapt high in the air, saying, "At least I have made you break the silence, and provoked you to anger!"

But Dominic calmly replied, "Not at all, for I have the authority to dispense from the rule. Nor is it blameworthy anger when I speak reproofs to evildoers."

Hearing that answer, the demon was obliged to flee.[3]

---

[3] Quoted in Drane, 145–46; the original language here and in other older translations throughout this book has been slightly adapted.

The Devil Takes a Tour of the Convent

One night Dominic was walking around the convent of
St. Sabina, making his rounds to guard his flock as any good
shepherd would do. He met the Enemy in the dormitory,
prowling around like a roaring lion, seeking someone to
devour (see 1 Pt 5:8).

Recognizing the Demon this time, the saint told him,
"You evil beast! What are you doing here?"

"I take care of my business," the Devil replied, "and keep
track of my gains."

"And what gains do you make in the dormitory?"

"Gain enough. I disturb the friars in many ways. First, I
take away sleep from those who desire to sleep so that they
can get out of bed promptly for early morning prayer. Then
I give excessive drowsiness to others, so that when the bell
rings to call them to prayer, either from weariness or laziness,
they don't get up. And if they do get up and assemble for
prayer, they do it unwillingly, and they say their office without devotion."

Then the saint took him into the church and asked,
"What do you gain here?"

"Much!" replied the Devil. "I make them come late and
leave early. I fill them with criticisms and distractions, so
that they do poorly whatever they have to do."

"And here?" asked Dominic, leading him into the din-
ing room.

"Who is it that doesn't eat either too much or too little?
Either they offend God by eating too much, or they injure
their health by eating too little."

Next the saint took him to the parlor, where the brothers were allowed to speak with lay visitors and to enjoy their
recreation. At this point, the Enemy began to laugh, and
leap, and jump about with malice, showing great pleasure.

"This place is all my own," he insisted. "Here they laugh
and joke and hear a thousand vain stories. Here they speak

idle words and grumble often about the rule of the order and their superiors. Whatever they may gain everywhere else, they lose here."

Finally, they came to the door of the chapter room, where the friars confessed their sins to one another and received penances. The Devil refused to enter the room. As he started to flee, he said, "This place is a hell to me. Here the friars accuse themselves of their faults and receive reproof and correction and absolution. What they have lost in every other place, they regain here!"

Then the evil spirit departed. Dominic was left to marvel at the snares and nets of the Tempter. Afterward, he had a long talk with his brothers, telling them what had happened and warning them to be on their guard.[4]

Even so, the saint's presence no doubt strengthened them as it did others. A university student who once served Mass with him said that when he kissed Dominic's hand, he could smell a heavenly fragrance. That fragrance, he insisted, had the power to deliver him from certain grave temptations that had been tormenting him.[5]

"Your Order Is My Ruin!"

A final anecdote from the early days of the Dominicans sums up the spiritual victories won by the saint's labors. Two of the brothers were walking along the road to the city of Bologna, Italy, to attend a great gathering of the entire order, not long before their founder died in 1221. They were met by a man who began walking with them and started up a conversation.

He asked why they were traveling. When they told him of the approaching assembly, he asked, "What is the business that's likely to be discussed?"

---

[4] Drane, 146–47.
[5] Drane, 203–4.

"The establishment of our brothers in new countries," one of the friars replied. "England and Hungary are among those countries proposed."

"And Greece as well," the other added, "and Germany, too, right?"

"Yes, that's right," said the first friar. "It's said that we'll soon be scattered across all these lands."

Then the stranger cried out in anguish and shouted, "Your religious order is my ruin!" He leapt into the air and disappeared. So the friars knew that he was the great Enemy of the human race—and that even he had been compelled to bear witness to the power that God had given the Dominicans to vanquish him.

- CHAPTER 11 -

ST. FRANCIS OF ASSISI
Soldier of Simplicity
(c. 1181–1226)

Stand, therefore, having fastened the belt of truth around your
waist, and having put on the breastplate of righteousness, and
having shod your feet with the equipment of the gospel of peace.
Ephesians 6:14–15

In Dominic's day, the task of thwarting the Enemy by renewing the Church was much too great a challenge for only one man and his followers, however numerous and victorious they might be. So the divine Commander commissioned another general, who rallied a new host of soldiers to fight. His name was Francis di Bernardone, and the Church has never seen a more colorful spiritual warrior.

Born just eleven years after Dominic in the Italian city of Assisi, Francis was the son of a wealthy silk merchant. He spent his early years living carelessly and extravagantly, seeking pleasure and glory. He was charming, handsome, courteous, and gallant, much loved among the young nobles of the city.

Around the age of twenty, Francis went off with the soldiers of his native city to battle the troops of its rival, Perugia. Assisi lost the battle, and he was taken prisoner for more than a year. After his release, he was ill for a time, and he began to have second thoughts about his way of life.

Nevertheless, when his health returned, the young man resolved to pursue a military career. He returned to the battles in 1205, but two dreams finally convinced him that he was fighting the wrong war. Christ had called him to His own army instead, to do battle with the ancient Enemy.

In his dream, Francis saw a vast hall with armor hanging along the walls, and on each piece was a cross. "These are for you and your soldiers," a voice announced. It was the divine summons to battle.

The Bitter Will Become Sweet

After a period of uncertainty, Francis began seeking God's will for his life through prayer and fasting.[1] Meanwhile, the Enemy tried to stop him through malicious deceit. One day as the young man was praying about his vocation, the Devil made him think of a woman who lived nearby who was terribly deformed. He threatened to make Francis look like her if the youth refused to abandon his pursuit of God's will.

But God spoke clearly to the young man, saying inwardly, "Francis, take the fleshly things you have loved in vain and exchange them for spiritual things. Acknowledge Me, and accept whatever bitterness I may give you, instead of the sweet things of this world. Consider yourself to be of no account. If you do these things, then what has been bitter to you will become sweet."

Soon after, Francis had his famous life-changing encounter with the leper. The details of the events that followed are well known, leading up to the young man's embrace of

---

[1] The incident about the demons besieging the Portiuncula is based on the account in *The Little Flowers of Saint Francis of Assisi*, trans. T. W. Arnold (London: Dent, 1909), 35–36. The episode in the church near Trevi is from Leo of Assisi, *Francis of Assisi: The Mirror of Perfection*, ed. Paul Sabatier, trans. Sebastian Evans (London: David Nutt, 1899), 98–99. All other anecdotes are based on the accounts in Thomas Celano, *Lives of Saint Francis of Assisi*, trans. A. G. Ferrers Howell (London: Methuen, 1908), 66–70, 152–53, 175–78, 205–6, 253–55.

poverty and preaching to spread the gospel of his new Commander. After attracting numerous disciples, he founded
the Order of Friars Minor ("little brothers") in 1209.

The Inner Battlefield

The first battles for Francis to win were the ones within his
own heart. The Enemy of his soul tried various tactics to
make him stumble. But each time, God gave the saint the
grace to remain firm.

Often the Devil attempted to instill in Francis a fear of
his malicious power. Seeking a place to pray alone at night,
the friar would sometimes find an empty church or another
deserted place. In the dark silence, the Enemy would press
in with distressing and even terrifying thoughts.

All alone there, one of his friars later reported, Francis "fought hand to hand with the Devil." For the Enemy
assaulted him not only with provocations to fear but also
with threats to his bodily safety. Sometimes the walls of
the buildings where he was praying would cave in or the
entire building would collapse.

But even though he faced such attacks completely alone,
Francis was undeterred. "God's valiant knight," the friar
concluded, "knowing that his Lord can do all things everywhere, did not yield to the terrors, but said in his heart, 'You
can no more brandish the weapons of wickedness here,
you Evil One, than if we were in public, with everyone gathered around.'"

Whatever the Lord Permits!

One night Francis was praying alone in the church of St. Peter
near the walled town of Trevi. Having finished his prayers,
he needed to rest. But he was prevented from going to sleep
because of the Devil's harassment. Diabolical thoughts filled
his mind and attempted to terrify him.

So the saint went out of the church, crossed himself, and said, "On behalf of God Almighty, I command you demons to do to my body whatever the Lord Jesus Christ permits you to do! For I'm ready to suffer anything He permits. After all, the greatest enemy I have is my own body, so you'll be avenging me of my most bitter adversary and foe!"

Immediately the fiendish thoughts ceased. The Enemy was dumbfounded and thwarted. Then Francis went back into the church, laid down, and slept in peace.

Temptations to Impurity

At the hermitage in Sartiano, the Devil planned a severe assault on Francis through temptation. One night while the friar was praying in his cell, the Enemy called to him, saying, "Francis! Francis! Francis!"

"What do you want?" the saint replied.

"There's no sinner in the world whom the Lord won't pardon if he turns from his sin. But whoever kills himself by hard penances will never find mercy for eternity."

God immediately revealed to Francis the strategy of the Enemy. He was trying to entice the friar to be spiritually lukewarm. But the Enemy failed. Realizing that his subtle attempt to conceal his efforts was ineffective, he tried another approach.

This time, he launched an all-out assault through temptation to lust. But it was all in vain. The holy man who had unmasked the craftiness of the spiritual temptation would not be tricked by the flesh.

The Devil presented Francis with a severe temptation to impurity, so the friar laid aside his habit and disciplined himself with the cord. But still the temptation would not leave him. So he went outside—it was midwinter—walked naked into the garden, and plunged into the deep snow.

Then, collecting the snow by handfuls, Francis made seven snowballs and set them out in front of himself. "Look!" he shouted. "This big one is your wife. These four are your two sons and two daughters. The other two are the servants you've had to hire to wait on them.

"Hurry up and find clothes for them all—they're dying of the cold! But if you're troubled by all the cares of having to provide for them, then maybe you should go back to serving God zealously as a friar, where you have only Him to serve!"

The Devil saw that he could not win. So he left in frustration, and Francis went back to his cell, glorifying God.

Moving a Mountain of Temptation

As the holiness of Francis grew deeper, so did his enmity with the old Serpent. The greater the anointing of the saint, the more subtle the temptations and the more violent the assaults the Devil sent his way. For even though Francis had proven himself a valiant warrior who had never yielded in the struggle for even an hour, the Devil sought relentlessly to wear down his victorious foe.

For this reason, the Enemy visited the saint with an extended season of extreme temptation of the spirit. But God had allowed it so that Francis might have a more glorious crown in heaven as his reward. The friar's situation was difficult and filled with grief. So he disciplined his body, prayed fervently, and shed many tears.

This season of adversity went on and on for two years. Then one day, when Francis was praying in Santa Maria di Portiuncula, in his spirit, he heard a voice saying, "Francis, if you will have faith like a grain of mustard seed, you will command a mountain to be removed, and it will be removed" (see Mt 17:20).

The saint replied, "Lord, which mountain is it that I should want to be removed?"

Then he heard the answer: "The mountain is your temptation."

So the friar replied with tears, "Lord, let it be to me according to your word" (see Lk 1:38). And right away, all the temptation was driven away. He was set free and completely at rest in his soul.

The Demon-Infested Pillow

From the day when Francis had been converted, he had sought to detach himself from the comforts of the world. For this reason, he had refused to sleep with a comforter or a feather pillow under his head. Even when he was sick or when strangers offered him more comfortable bedding, he never suspended this discipline.

But one night at the hermitage of Greccio, when he was suffering more than usual from the pain of a chronic eye ailment, he was compelled, against his will, to accept a pillow. Yet at the matins prayers of the first night, he called his companion to his room.

"Brother, I haven't been able to sleep tonight," he said, "nor to remain upright in prayer. My body trembles, my knees give out from under me, and my whole body is out of gear, as if I had eaten bread made out of weeds. I believe the Devil has infested this pillow that I have under my head. Take it away! I don't want the Devil at my head any longer."

His companion, sympathizing with his spiritual father's complaint, caught the pillow when Francis tossed it to him. He took it out of the room to put it away, but immediately he was unable to speak. His mind was so oppressed and bound up by a sense of horror that he stopped in his tracks and could not even move his arms or legs.

After a little while, Francis, who realized what had happened, called to him. When he did, the brother was released. He returned to the room and told the saint about his experience.

Francis said to him, "Last night, when I was saying the evening prayers, I knew without a doubt that the Devil would visit my cell. Our foe is quite crafty and subtle. When he can't hurt us within our souls, he gives our bodies good reason to complain."

Francis Watches Out for His Brothers

Francis was concerned with far more than the Devil's assaults against him personally. God had given him a flock to watch over—the men who came to him to join his order. And the spiritual warfare in which Francis engaged necessarily involved his brothers as well.

Sometimes the saint could actually see evil spirits harassing the friars or riding on their backs. But in response to his prayers, the Lord would deliver them. One night while he was in fervent prayer at the Portiuncula, God showed him that the whole place was surrounded and besieged by an army of demons. Nevertheless, the brothers were so holy that the unclean spirits could find no entrance.

As the unclean spirits persevered, however, one of the friars was provoked to anger and impatience against one of his brothers. He pondered how he could falsely accuse him and take revenge on him. In doing so, he gave the Enemy a way to gain admittance.

Right away, while Francis was watching, one of the demons entered the place and jumped on the brother's neck, like a winning wrestler making his move on the loser. So Francis, alarmed that a wolf had attacked one of his sheep, called for the friar to come to him. The friar came running obediently.

Francis instructed him to reveal immediately the poisonous hatred against his neighbor that he was harboring. He told him that such hatred had made him vulnerable to the Enemy's assault. The brother was terrified to realize that Francis had read his heart, but he confessed everything.

When he had acknowledged his fault, begged forgiveness, and received a penance, he was absolved of his sin. Then Francis saw the demon flee away. The friar gave thanks to God and to Francis, and he persevered in holiness for the rest of his life.

Delivered From the Fear of Demons

A brother named Angelo had a great fear of the demons because he had heard about the terrible battles that Francis had fought with them. One day the saint summoned the friar, and he confessed this weakness to his spiritual father. He begged to be permitted a companion at night to sleep in his cell with him, because his fears were greater and more distressing in the night than in the day.

The saint replied, "Timid soul! Why do you fear such weak and insignificant enemies? As you know well, their strength and power are under God's control.

"So that you may experience this reality, I command you to climb this night, alone, to the pinnacle of the nearby mountain. Once you are there, cry out in a loud voice, 'Proud demons, come to me now, all of you, and let loose all your fury on me. Do to me whatever you can!'"

The brother was no doubt terrified. But he humbly obeyed this order of his superior. When he did, no demons appeared. So he was delivered forever from his great fear.[2]

Francis Wants to Avoid Vainglory

One day Francis was preaching in the fortress of San Gemini, in the diocese of Narni. A holy, God-fearing man of that town was hosting the saint and three other friars in his home

---

[2] Francis of Assisi, *Works of the Seraphic Father St. Francis of Assisi* (London: R. Washbourne, 1882), 231.

for a meal. But the man was terribly burdened by his wife's condition, known to all the town: She was tormented by a demon.

The host asked Francis to cast the demon out of his wife, for he believed that by the holy man's merits, she could be delivered. But the friar hesitated. He feared that the people would treat him as a celebrity if he did such a thing.

Finally, however, Francis was moved by compassion for the woman, and he realized that it would be to God's glory for her to be freed. So he yielded to the fervent requests of the people. He told the three friars that they were to station themselves in the four corners of the house to pray, keeping the demon surrounded with prayers. Perhaps it was also to clarify that God was answering not just his prayers but the prayers of others as well.

When he had finished praying, Francis went to the woman, filled with the power of the Holy Spirit. She was weeping horribly, miserably tormented. The saint said, "In the name of our Lord Jesus Christ, I command you, demon, to leave her, and don't bother her ever again. You must obey."

He had hardly finished speaking the words when the demon rushed out of her with a beastly roar. At first, the saint thought he was tricked because the demon had obeyed so promptly without resistance and the woman had been healed so quickly. And when he left the house, he felt ashamed. He realized he should never have worried that he might become puffed up with vanity for having cast out the demon. God had made it utterly clear that it was His power accomplishing the miracle and Francis was just His instrument.

How Francis Tested a Demon-Possessed Woman

Once at Città di Castello, a demon-possessed woman was brought to the house where Francis was staying. She remained outside, gnashing her teeth, contorting her face, and bellowing, sounding much like an elephant trumpeting. Both men and women from the city came to Francis, begging him to cast out the demon. It had long tormented the woman and disturbed them all by its roaring.

The woman didn't know what the saint looked like, so he decided to put her to a test to see whether she was indeed possessed by an unclean spirit or only deceiving everyone. Francis sent one of the other brothers into her house, instead of going himself, to see how she would respond.

When the other brother appeared, the demon, speaking through her, began to mock him. It knew that he was not Francis. Meanwhile, Francis was outside her house praying.

When he had finished, the saint went into the house. Immediately the woman began to shake and to roll on the ground. The spirit was reacting to God's power flowing through Francis.

In this way, he knew that she was truly possessed by a demon, so he addressed it: "I command you, unclean spirit, leave her! You must obey." Then the demon came out of her right away without hurting her and left in a fury.

Demons Cast Out of a City

Francis' word had authority over demons, and the power of his word was so effective that it could be transmitted through others when he himself was absent. One day he happened to come to the city of Arezzo when the community there was torn by internal strife. A destructive civil war seemed imminent.

The man of God chose a lodging outside the city walls. As he gazed at the city, he could see demons exulting over it, inflaming the citizens to seek mutual destruction. So he called Brother Sylvester, a godly man of worthy simplicity, and gave him this instruction.

"Go before the city," he said. "There, on behalf of Almighty God, command the demons to leave it as quickly as possible!"

The humble brother made no objection and hurried to obey. When he reached the gates of the city, he sought God's favor by offering Him praise. Then he cried out toward the city, "On behalf of God, and by order of our father Francis, depart and go far away from here, all you demons!"

Soon afterward, peace was restored to the city and just laws were observed, resulting in great tranquility. When the day came for Francis to begin his preaching, he opened with these words: "I speak to you as to those who were formerly in subjection to the Devil and in the bonds of demons. But I know you have now been set free by the prayers of a certain poor man."

By bringing tranquility to the city through divine assistance, the friar had proven the truth of the Apostle's words: "The God of peace will soon crush Satan under your feet" (Rom 16:20). In a sense, that declaration sums up the whole life of Francis: He fought the good fight—valiantly, tirelessly—so that others could be at peace with God, with themselves, and with others. In doing so, he crushed the Enemy's head beneath him.

- CHAPTER 12 -

ST. CATHERINE OF SIENA
Wisdom's Champion
(1347–1380)

If you have bitter jealousy and selfish ambition in your hearts, do not boast and be false to the truth. This wisdom is not such as comes down from above, but is earthly, unspiritual, devilish. For where jealousy and selfish ambition exist, there will be disorder and every vile practice. But the wisdom from above is first pure, then peaceable, open to reason, full of mercy and good fruits.

James 3:14–17

Not long before he died in 1226, St. Francis prophesied that the day was fast approaching when the Church would endure a great schism, with a false antipope who opposed the true pope. "There will be great trials and afflictions," he was reported to have said. "Perplexities and dissensions, both spiritual and temporal, will abound; the charity of many will grow cold, and the malice of the wicked will increase. The devils will have unusual power." [1]

The prophecy was apparently fulfilled in 1378 when the Church suffered a schism that would last almost forty years. The spiritual causes and consequences of that tragedy were incalculable. Corruption and sexual immorality were rampant among the clergy, the religious orders once

---

[1] *Seraphic Father*, 248–50.

again needed reform, and among lay people, doctrinal ignorance, heresy, weak faith, and lax morals were common. But spiritual tribulations were only one aspect of the great misery in western Europe of the fourteenth century.

In the early years of the century, rapid population growth and harvest failures led to large-scale famines across the continent. Midcentury, the bubonic plague—"the Black Death," as it was called—swept across Europe, wiping out a third of the population and devastating society at every level. In 1337, England and France began the so-called Hundred Years War, which killed many thousands more.

The words of Francis most certainly rang true: The devils did indeed have unusual power.

Catherine, Spiritual Champion

Into this tormented age, God sent a remarkable woman named Catherine Benincasa, born in Siena, Italy, in 1347. As a young woman, she consecrated herself to Christ and became a lay follower of St. Dominic. She became in many ways the greatest spiritual champion of her time.

Catherine spent countless hours in prayer, contemplation, and spiritual discipline, achieving majestic heights in mystical experience. Her spiritual writings have nourished Christians of every generation since her time, and she was one of the first women to be declared a Doctor of the Church. Yet Catherine was even more than a mystical teacher: Her enlightening conversations with God and her private victories over the demons sent her back out into the world around her.

This tireless young woman cared for the poor, the prisoners, and the victims of leprosy, cancer, and even the Black Death. She provided spiritual counsel to the many souls who came to her for wisdom. Even princes and popes sought her advice, and she became one of the most influential women on the continent. Often she made it her mission to reconcile political and military adversaries and win peace.

In all these ways, in Catherine, the Devil found a formidable opponent.[2]

The Devil and the Child

Catherine's first biographer, Blessed Raymond of Capua, was her spiritual director and learned about her childhood through interviews with her family members. He reports that at the age of seven, she consecrated her virginity to Christ. She at first kept that fact to herself because her family would not have understood why.

When Catherine grew old enough for her parents to start thinking about finding her a husband, she found herself in a difficult situation: She wanted to obey her parents, but she had no interest in making herself attractive for a potential mate. By then, Raymond tells us, the Devil was already targeting her with temptations to forsake her vow.

The Enemy of salvation could see that the snares he had laid to destroy Catherine were futile. She had only sought more fervently a refuge in the bosom of her heavenly Spouse, loving Him more than ever. So Satan erected obstacles for her in her own home and sought to bind her to the world through the fierceness of her family's persecutions.

The Devil inspired her relatives to make up their minds that she must marry. But enlightened by heaven, Catherine only increased her prayers, meditations, and discipline. She avoided the company of men, proving in every way the firmness of her resolution never to give to a simple mortal the heart that had been accepted by the King of kings.

Her parents tried every strategy they could imagine to overcome her resistance. But when Catherine cut off her

---

[2] The following accounts are drawn from the early biography by Raymond of Capua, *Life of St. Catherine of Siena*, trans. Mother Regis Hamilton (New York: P. J. Kenedy, 1862), 36–38, 46–47, 67–72.

hair and covered her head, the family was furious. They pun-
ished her with harsh words and even harsher treatment.

They told her that she would have no peace until she
consented to marriage, and they found an eligible young
bachelor whom they intended for her to marry. They forced
her to perform all the housework, hoping that the drudgery
filling her days would leave her no time to pray. They even
dismissed the kitchen maid and pressed Catherine to take
on the dirtiest tasks she had performed.

The Devil thought that through all these tactics, he
would at last defeat Catherine in this struggle. But instead,
he himself was again vanquished. Instead of yielding, the
young woman became stronger with the help of grace.
The Holy Spirit had taught her to erect a little cell in the
interior of her soul, and she resolved never to leave it, even
when exterior occupations pressed upon her. As Our Lord
said, "The kingdom of God is within you" (see Lk 17:21).

Eventually, Catherine's parents resigned themselves to
recognize her consecration as a bride of Christ. But when
she began to practice various forms of strict self-discipline,
her mother in particular was horrified. The old Serpent
renewed his attacks on the young woman through her
mother's constant efforts to hinder her acts of penance.

As Raymond tells us, the Devil was able to inspire the
mother because "she had a greater love for her daughter's
body than for her soul." But once again, Catherine found
ways to honor her parents while remaining obedient to
God. In time, her mother accepted God's will for Catherine. Because of her daughter's persistence, the Enemy of her
soul had lost again.

A Renewed Assault

Even so, the Devil refused to give up. As Catherine engaged
in rigorous penances, he found new ways to assault her.
Blessed Raymond reports:

The old Serpent saw Catherine, so young, mounting to such a high degree of perfection. He feared that with her salvation, the salvation of many others would be secured, and she would assist the Church by her virtues and her teaching. For this reason, in his hellish malice he sought every possible way to seduce her. But the God of mercy, who permitted these attacks in order to increase the glory of His bride, gave her such excellent weapons for combat that the war proved more profitable to her than peace.

The first weapon God gave her was in response to her prayer for gaining fortitude. He told Catherine:

"Daughter, if you wish to acquire fortitude, you must imitate Me. I could have, by My divine power, stopped Satan's efforts and taken other means of overcoming them. But I desired to instruct you by My example and teach you to overcome by means of the Cross.

"If you wish to become powerful against your enemies, take the Cross for your defense. Hasn't My apostle told you that I ran with joy to the cruel and shameful death of Mount Calvary [see Heb 12:2]? So choose to have trials and afflictions. Don't just endure them with patience; embrace them with delight."

When the King of heaven and earth had armed Catherine in this way to defend His cause, He permitted the enemy to advance and assail her. The demons attacked her on every side, making unprecedented efforts to overthrow her. They began with the most humiliating temptations, presenting them to her imagination, not only during sleep but in disturbing apparitions intended to defile her eyes and ears. They tormented her in a thousand ways. Catherine responded to the temptations by doubling her penances. For a while, she even lengthened her prayer vigils until she denied herself all sleep.

Still the Enemy pressed in. The demons appeared to her under the form of people who came to pity and advise her:

"Why, poor little one, will you torture yourself this way, and so uselessly? Why use all these penances? Do you really think you'll be able to continue them? Won't you destroy your body this way and become guilty of suicide?

"It's better to renounce such foolishness before you become its victim. You can still enjoy the world. You're young, and your body would quickly recover its strength.

"You desire to please God. But remember that among the saints were many who were married: Sarah, Rebecca, Leah, and Rachel. Why be so imprudent as to select a way of life in which you can't persevere?"

In response, Catherine simply prayed and said, "I trust in the arm of the Lord, and not in mine." That was the only reaction the demons could get from her.

Humility Was Her Armor

Catherine made it her general rule, when fighting against such temptations, never to dispute with the Enemy, because he relies heavily on vanquishing us by the subtlety of his reasoning. So Satan laid aside his reasoning and adopted a new method of attack.

The demons began pursuing the young woman with screams. They invited her to take part in their abominations. It did her no good to close her eyes and ears; she was unable to get rid of such horrible specters.

To complete her affliction, her divine Spouse, who usually came to visit and comfort her, seemed to abandon her without any relief. Her soul was plunged into a profound sadness. Yet, even then, she refused to relax her penances. By her humility, she confounded the Prince of Darkness.

During this time, Catherine concluded that her room was infested with impure spirits. So she spent as much time in the church as possible. The hellish obsessions tormented her less when she was there.

This trial continued for several days. One day when she had returned from the church and was praying, a ray of the Holy Spirit beamed upon her soul and reminded her that she had recently prayed for the gift of fortitude and that God had told her how to obtain it. She immediately realized the cause of this frightening temptation and resolved to bear it with holy courage, as long as it pleased her divine Spouse.

Then one evil spirit, more malicious than the others, said to her, "Poor miserable soul! What are you about to undertake? Can you spend your whole life in this way? We will torture you to death, unless you obey us!"

Catherine remembered the instruction she had received and replied, "I have chosen sufferings for my consolation. Not only will it not be difficult for me; it will actually be delightful to undergo similar afflictions and even greater ones for the love of my Jesus, as long as His Majesty wills it."

Jesus Appears to Catherine

In that instant, the demons fled in overwhelming shame, and a great light from above descended into her room, filling it with heavenly brightness. In the midst of its radiance, she saw our Lord Jesus Christ, appearing as He had appeared on the Cross, when He opened heaven with His sacred Blood.

"Catherine, My daughter," He said, "consider how I have suffered for you, and it will never be painful for you to suffer for Me." Then He took on a less sorrowful form in order to comfort Catherine, and He spoke to her of the victory that she had just gained.

Nevertheless, she, like St. Anthony, said to Him, "Lord, where were You when my heart was so tormented?"

"I was right there in the midst of your heart."

"Lord, You are the eternal truth, and I humbly bow before Your Majesty. But how can I believe that You were in my heart when it was filled with such detestable thoughts?"

"Did these thoughts and temptations give you pleasure or pain?"

"An extreme pain and sadness."

"You were sad and in suffering because I was hidden in the midst of your heart. Had I been absent, these thoughts would have penetrated your heart and filled you with pleasure. But My presence rendered them unbearable to you. You wished to repel them because they horrified you. It was because you didn't succeed that you were burdened with sadness.

"I acted in your soul. I defended you against your enemy. I was inside you, and I permitted these attacks from outside you only to the extent that they could prove useful for your salvation. When the period that I had set for the combat was finished, I sent My beams of light, and the shadows of hell were scattered because they could not resist the light."

The vision disappeared, but Catherine remained absorbed in what Jesus had said to her, with a joy and sweetness beyond words. After that time, He appeared to her more frequently and more intimately.

Demons Flee From Catherine

After Catherine became a Third Order Dominican, her reputation for holiness grew. People began seeking her out for counsel and even to perform miracles. Sometimes those possessed by demons were healed by her prayer or even just her touch.[3]

---

[3] The following anecdote is based on an eyewitness account by Francesco Maltevolti, a young nobleman who was present in the city, as described in F. A. Forbes, *Saint Catherine of Siena* (repr., Rockford, Ill.: TAN Books, 1998), 63–67.

One day, she was staying at the fortress town of Rocca d'Orcia, hosted by the Countess Bianchina, on a mission of peace. Twelve men came to town carrying a man bound with ropes and shackles on his hands and feet. They told the people he was possessed by a demon and had ferociously injured several people, biting and ripping with his teeth the flesh of anyone who came close to him.

The twelve men had agreed to bring him to Rocca d'Orcia from his own village only if he were securely restrained. Even so, they had found it a daunting task to get him there. When they laid him out on the plaza, he was still screaming and roaring with a voice that scarcely sounded human. He tried to bite anyone nearby, looking wildly at all those around.

Word was sent to the countess, asking that she bring the young woman to the plaza. The hostess convinced her to come but without telling her why, because Catherine was usually hesitant to become involved in cases of possession. Perhaps the young woman wished to avoid taking the place of an exorcist who had been duly appointed for such work.

When Catherine, the countess, and most of the household appeared in the plaza, the demoniac began screaming horribly and writhing furiously, trying to escape his shackles. The crowd was terrified, but Catherine said to her hostess, "What has this poor man done, that he should be so cruelly bound? For the love of God, bid them set him free. Don't you see how he's suffering?"

Then she turned to the twelve men who had brought him. "Dearest brothers," she entreated them, "don't leave this creature of God in such pain. Loose him and give him some refreshment. There's nothing the matter with him."

"Lady," they replied, "he has injured several of our people fearfully. Still, if you will promise to remain near us, we will set him free at your command."

Then Catherine drew close to the poor man and gave the command that he be freed in the name of Jesus Christ.

At those words, the man lay still and allowed the others to unbind him.

"Now lift him up," Catherine instructed them, "and give him some refreshment. You'll see that when he's had some food, he'll be no longer the same man."

As soon as the man was set on his feet, he came and knelt down before Catherine. She blessed him with the Sign of the Cross. He could remember nothing that had happened, and he was amazed to find himself at Rocca d'Orcia instead of his own village. They gave him food, and then he left the castle, completely healed, with the men who had brought him there. Never again was he tormented by the demons.

The Pickpocket

Catherine became so accustomed to the Devil's assaults that she gave him a nickname. She called him "Pickpocket" because he tried to snatch souls.

Blessed Raymond tells how the old Serpent would sometimes become so furious over the harvest of souls she was reaping for God that he would push her into the fire, with many of her friends watching. They would scream and weep, trying to get her out of the flames.

But Catherine would get up smiling, without any burn marks on her skin or clothing. "Don't be frightened," she told them, "of the old Pickpocket!"

One day when she was returning with companions from Rome to Siena, riding on a donkey, she was thrown from the saddle headlong into a deep ravine. But they found Catherine lying on the ground, laughing merrily. She said it had simply been a blow from "Pickpocket."

She stood up and the party continued their journey. A little farther down the road, the Devil threw her off her mount again, and she ended up in the mud with the donkey on top of her. But she brushed if off with a witty remark to mock the Enemy: "This donkey is warming up the side that always hurts me!"

At this point, her friends urged her not to get back on the donkey but to walk the rest of the way, so she set out on foot. But Satan kept pulling her, first one way and then the other. If her companions had not held on to her, she might well have fallen many times.

All the while, Catherine was laughing at her Enemy, treating him with the mockery and contempt he deserved.[4]

Diabolical Retaliation

The last two years of Catherine's brief life were lived in the miserable shadow of the schism that St. Francis had prophesied. From 1309 to 1377, a series of seven popes, all Frenchmen and dominated by the French crown, had maintained residence in Avignon, France, rather than Rome. She had been instrumental in convincing the last of these to return his residence to Rome.

But just as Catherine was rejoicing that the Bishop of Rome was at last living in Rome, as he should have been, the Church was torn in half by the conflict of two parties. One was in support of the French-dominated clergy and the other in support of the Romans. Finally the French cardinals separated from their brothers in 1378 and elected an anti-Pope.

Catherine was deeply grieved by these events, and in the following months, she sought to win influential secular rulers to the side of the true pope. She was living in Rome at the time, in a house on the Via Chiara. While she was there, in 1379, she became convinced that demons were harassing her for having helped obtain the return of the papacy to Rome. She described the experience in a letter:

---

[4] Blessed Raymond of Capua, *The Life of St. Catherine*, trans. George Lamb (repr., Rockford, Ill.: TAN Books, 2003), 115, 373–74.

And after a little while, the terror of the demons began in such a way that they utterly stupefied me; mad with rage against me that I, a worm, had been the means of wresting from their hands what they had long time possessed in Holy Church. So great was my terror and bodily pain that I wanted to fly from the study and go into the chapel, as though the study had caused the pain. I rose up, therefore, and being unable to walk, I leaned upon my [spiritual] son, Barduccio.

But I was immediately flung down; and lying there, it seemed to me that my soul had left my body; but not in the way that once happened to me, when I had tasted the bliss of the immortals, enjoying Supreme Good together with them. This was quite different.[5]

Catherine's body became lifeless, and her companion thought she was dead. But her mind was quite conscious, so she began to pray inwardly for God's help, not only in her immediate distress, but also in the greater troubles that were afflicting the Church.

By now, her other friends had gathered around, concluding that she had in fact died. But God spoke to her, affirming that He would answer her prayers. The terror of the demons subsided.

Catherine's body slowly revived, and she was brought to her room to recover. But her heart was still filled with anguish, and the battle was not yet over. The unclean spirits attempted to convince her that she herself was actually one of them:

When they carried me upstairs, the room seemed full of demons, who began to wage another battle against me, the most terrible that I ever endured, striving to make me believe and see that I was not she who was in the body,

---

[5] Alice Curtayne, *Saint Catherine of Siena* (repr., Rockford, Ill.: TAN Books, 1980), 193.

but rather an impure spirit. I then called on the divine aid with sweet tenderness.[6]

For two days and nights, the attack continued. The assault on her mind lifted, but the diabolical violence against her body continued.

Finally, when she was able to attend Mass on the Feast of the Purification of Mary, she received a revelation from God that her prayerful suffering was effective. Through it, she was "doing what the holy martyrs did with their blood," and she hoped to see before long "the redemption of [God's] people." But in her report of these events, she concluded, "My life is hanging by a thread."[7]

Indeed it was. She barely survived into the next year, feeling as if she somehow bore responsibility for the schism and its continuance. One day in church during the Lenten season of 1380, she collapsed and had to be carried out. From then until her death not long after, she was paralyzed from the waist down.

On April 29, she passed on to her heavenly reward. But the many miracles that occurred among the throngs that came to view her body and mourn her passing made manifest that she had indeed won her battle with the Enemy of her soul. Her heroic example, her wise teaching, and her powerful intercession have helped countless others since then to do the same.

---

[6] Curtayne, 194.

[7] Curtayne, 195.

- CHAPTER 13 -

ST. IGNATIUS LOYOLA
Seasoned Strategist
(1491–1556)

Put on the whole armor of God, that you may
be able to stand against the wiles of the Devil.
Ephesians 6:11

The violent internal tribulations of the Church in St. Catherine's time eventually bore their bitter fruit in the Prot-
estant revolt against Rome in the sixteenth century. Martin
Luther was only the first of many who broke decisively with
the Catholic Church to establish a bewildering assortment
of new religions and political alliances. The ancient Enemy of
the Church exulted, both in the confusion and corruption that
had contributed to the multiple schisms and in the shattering
of even the semblance of Christian unity.

Into this desperate situation, God sent a man named
Ignatius, a Spanish knight from the Basque country, born in
1491 in the village of Loyola. From an early age, Ignatius
imagined himself as a soldier. He loved martial exercises and
longed for glory.[1]

---

[1] Most of the following account is based on two sources: St. Ignatius of
Loyola, *The Autobiography of St. Ignatius*, ed. J. F. X. O'Conor (New York:
Benziger, 1900), and Father Genelli, S.J., in *Life of St. Ignatius of Loyola*
(repr., Rockford, Ill.: TAN Books, 1988), 55–59.

The young man joined the army at the age of seventeen. He fought in a number of battles without injury, demonstrating leadership and diplomatic skills within the ranks. But at the Battle of Pamplona, a few months after his twenty-ninth birthday, a cannonball wounded one of his legs and broke the other one.

While convalescing from the surgery he underwent for his injuries, Ignatius began a season of spiritual reading and contemplation that led to his conversion. He decided to serve as a soldier of Christ rather than an earthly commander. When he had recovered enough to travel, he visited a Benedictine monastery at Santa Maria de Montserrat and hung his sword and dagger there before an image of the Blessed Virgin. His lifelong spiritual combat had begun.

A Perplexing Vision

Ignatius next spent four months in severe penance and caring for the sick in a hospital in the little town of Manresa, not far from Montserrat. While there, he had a perplexing vision that would reoccur in the days to come, even after he had taken up residence in a cave near the town in order to engage in a prolonged spiritual retreat. The saint described it later in life this way, speaking of himself in the third person:

> It was while he was living at the hospital at Manresa that the following strange event took place. Very frequently on a clear moonlit night there appeared in the courtyard before him an indistinct shape which he could not see clearly enough to tell what it was. Yet it appeared so symmetrical and beautiful that his soul was filled with pleasure and joy as he gazed at it.
>
> It had something of the form of a serpent with glittering eyes, and yet they were not eyes. He felt an indescribable joy steal over him at the sight of this object. The oftener he saw it, the greater was the consolation he

derived from it, and when the vision left him, his soul was filled with sorrow and sadness.

Up to this period he had remained in a constant state of tranquility and consolation, without any interior knowledge of the trials that beset the spiritual life. But during the time that the vision lasted, sometimes for days, or a little previous to that time, his soul was violently agitated by a thought that brought him no little uneasiness.[2]

Satan, eager to turn the young man away from his intentions, began a fierce assault. The Enemy whispered to him:

"How can you keep up for seventy years these practices which you have begun?"

Knowing that this thought was a temptation of the Evil One, he expelled it by this answer: "Can you, wretched one, promise me even one hour of life?"

In this manner he overcame the temptation, and his soul was restored to peace.[3]

Interior Conflicts

After this assault, a long series of alternating consolations and desolations followed.

Shortly after the temptation just spoken of, he began to experience great changes in his soul. At one time he was deprived of all consolation, so that he found no pleasure in vocal prayer, in hearing Mass, or in any spiritual exercise. At another, on the contrary, he suddenly felt as if all sorrow and desolation were taken from him, experiencing the relief of one from whose shoulders a heavy cloak had suddenly been lifted.

On noticing all this, he was surprised, wondering what could be the import of these changes which he had never

---

[2] *Autobiography of St. Ignatius*, 40–42.

[3] *Autobiography of St. Ignatius*, 42.

before experienced, and he said to himself, "What new kind of life is this upon which I am entering?"[4]

As soon as Ignatius had overcome the revolt of his flesh against his spirit, he would face a more subtle temptation: to dwell with self-satisfaction on the merits he had gained by his penances. Since his health was bad, the Devil tried to persuade him that he should go ahead and die happily, since he would go straight to heaven.

At other times, Ignatius would suffer from scrupulosity. He was deeply depressed and caused his conscience to wallow in confusion and uncertainty. At one point, he even considered suicide. He developed a feeling of extreme disgust for the way of life he had adopted, with a strong temptation to go back to his old ways, leaving behind the interior martyrdom that had seemed so fruitless.

After ten months of such strenuous spiritual combat, Ignatius finally won the victory.

> One day he went to the Church of St. Paul, situated about a mile from Manresa. Near the road is a stream, on the bank of which he sat, and gazed at the deep waters flowing by. While seated there, the eyes of his soul were opened. He did not have any special vision, but his mind was enlightened on many subjects, spiritual and intellectual. So clear was this knowledge that from that day everything appeared to him in a new light. Such was the abundance of this light in his mind that all the divine helps received, and all the knowledge acquired up to his sixty-second year, were not equal to it.
>
> From that day he seemed to be quite another man, and possessed of a new intellect. This illumination lasted a long time.[5]

---

[4] Autobiography of St. Ignatius, 43.
[5] Autobiography of St. Ignatius, 56–57.

Nevertheless, the perplexing vision of a creature with glittering eyes soon returned. Having been enlightened, Ignatius could finally understand what it truly was.

> While kneeling in thanksgiving for this grace, there appeared to him that object which he had often seen before, but had never understood. It seemed to be something most beautiful, and, as it were, gleaming with many eyes. This is how it always appeared. There was a cross near which he was praying, and he noticed that near the cross the vision had lost some of its former beautiful color. He understood from this that the apparition was the work of the Devil, and whenever the vision appeared to him after that, as it did several times, he dispelled it with his staff.[6]

In his description of the vision's first occurrence, Ignatius had noted that the figure looked something like "a serpent with glittering eyes." Here he noted again the dazzling eyes. According to tradition, Lucifer was the kind of angel known as a seraph, and the seraphim appeared to Ezekiel as figures covered with eyes (see Ez 10:12).

Perhaps the suggestion here is that the young man was seeing the many eyes of the fallen seraph, the ancient Serpent himself. And since "Satan disguises himself as an angel of light" (2 Cor 11:14), it should be no wonder that the figure was radiant and that the vision gave the spiritual novice a deceptive sense of pleasure.

The Spiritual Exercises

Out of this season of inner warfare came one of the most effective books on spiritual battle strategy ever written: *The Spiritual Exercises*. Most of the work was composed while Ignatius was in the cave, and his struggles to discern the

---

[6] *Autobiography of St. Ignatius*, 57–58.

true source of various spiritual experiences during this time helped him share what he had learned.

In the *Exercises*, Ignatius sought to present "certain operations of the mind and heart . . . which are employed in order to free the soul from its irregular affections, and so to put it in the way of knowing and embracing the will of God toward it." Among those operations are "the examination of conscience, meditation, contemplation, mental and vocal prayer." [7] The work is characterized by a frequent use of the imagination to approach spiritual truths.

In addition to his "Rules for the Discernment of Spirits," which offer principles for evaluating spiritual experiences, Ignatius provides an extended meditation called "The Two Standards," or banners in battle. One standard belongs to the wicked hosts of Lucifer, and the other belongs to the army of Jesus Christ. Each of us must choose under which standard we will fight and serve.

The concluding words of his description of Lucifer and his minions are sobering: "Look on yourself. Be astonished at having given way so often and so easily to the temptations of the Enemy; weep over your folly and your past weakness, and resolve to be wiser and more courageous for the future." [8]

The book was not published until many years later, in 1548. By then, Ignatius had engaged the Devil in many other fields of combat—and not only within his soul.

Accusations and Acquittals

After his time at Manresa, Ignatius studied at the universities of Barcelona, Alcalá, and Salamanca. The Enemy was busy during those years as well: The saint was vehemently criticized, persecuted, and accused of preaching heresy, though he was exonerated of that charge.

---

[7] St. Ignatius of Loyola, *The Spiritual Exercises of Saint Ignatius; or Manresa* (repr., Rockford, Ill.: TAN Books, 1999), 1.

[8] *Spiritual Exercises*, 128.

Ignatius was quite persuasive in winning his fellow students to imitate his radical commitment to God. His enemies were dumbfounded at the many followers he gained, and they concluded that he was calling on the Devil through magic to bewitch them. So he was denounced to the tribunal of the Spanish Inquisition as a sorcerer. But eventually he was acquitted of those charges as well.

In 1534, he received his master of arts and founded the Society of Jesus, whose initial ranks were filled by his fellow students. The men were eventually ordained, and the society received papal approval in 1540. Before long, the Jesuits, as they were called, were sending out missionaries—not just throughout Europe but even to other continents—to push back the darkness of ignorance, heresy, and lukewarm religion.

The Demons' Formidable Enemy

The autobiography of Ignatius modestly omits the miracles that he performed in the course of his mission work. But after his death, his associates were formally examined about his sanctity as a part of his canonization proceedings. Multiple witnesses spoke of his ongoing spiritual combat and his power over evil spirits.

One Pietro Ribadeneira was juridically examined at Madrid in the year 1595. He declared that he could affirm the sanctity of the man "because of the great hatred which the Devil always had against Father Ignatius, and the continual persecutions which he moved against him. . . . When the members of the society were together without Father Ignatius, they had great peace and tranquility, but upon his arrival the Devil out of hatred toward him immediately roused some storm." [9]

---

[9] This account and the following ones from the saint's canonization procedures are drawn from Antonio Francesco Mariani, *The Life of St. Ignatius Loyola, Founder of the Jesuits* (London: Thomas Richardson and Son, 1849), vol. 2, 57.

Just as a demon had once said that he knew the Apostle Paul (see Acts 19:15), more than once, an evil spirit spoke of Ignatius as a formidable spiritual opponent. Ribadeneira reported:

> Father Lainez has also testified that he saw at Padua a miserable soldier possessed by the Devil, who though he had never known Father Ignatius, described him so true to life, and so naturally, that it was miraculous, and said that he was his greatest enemy in the world. This was confirmed by the words of another demon in Rome, who had invaded the body of a youth named Matthew, who was afterwards delivered by Ignatius. For upon the present witness saying that that father would soon return and drive him away from that body, he shrieked out and bid him not to name Ignatius, for he was his greatest enemy in the world.[10]

A similar affirmation was made by yet another demon at Trapani in Sicily, immediately after Ignatius died, according to the testimony of several ecclesiastical and civil officials who reported the incident to Rome.

Help From Heaven

In 1556, having "fought the good fight" (1 Tm 4:7), Ignatius finished his race and received his heavenly crown. But he continued his spiritual combat for the sake of those still on earth. The testimony in the cause for his canonization provides some remarkable accounts.

*   *   *   *

Four noble ladies named Lodovica Fontana, Francesca, Anna Brancolini, and Livia, daughter of Alberto Fontana,

---

[10] Mariani, 57–58.

and their nephews, all connected both by blood and friend-
ship, lived in Modena. Lodovica was married to Paolo Gui-
doni; Anna was unmarried, and Francesca and Livia were
virgins of the society of St. Ursula. By their virtuous examples, they had gained the esteem of the whole city, but this
admiration was converted into pity when the Devil griev-
ously tormented their bodies, which he had got possession of.

Their possession began with terrible maladies, which
changed their character and altered into other and different disorders, to the astonishment of the doctors. Sometimes they got quite well and strong and then, again, were
brought to the point of death. Sometimes by the application
of blessed water or oil, the disorder forsook one part of their
bodies and fastened on another.

They were tempted to self-destruction. They fled to quiet
parts of the house and dashed their heads against the walls
or the ground till the noise of their blows brought someone to the spot. Once Lodovica ran to the top of the house,
intending to throw herself down. But when, by God's mercy,
her husband realized it in sufficient time to thwart the plan,
the Devil dashed her on the ground so that she remained for
some time as if dead.

Their chief pleasure had formerly been found in prayer,
but now they could not pray without the greatest difficulty.
If they went to hear Mass, they generally fainted when it
began. When they went to confession, they lost the power
of speech and put out their tongues to ridicule the priests.

Sometimes they also broke out into blasphemous or vul-
gar words. What is still more painful to modest women, they
were strongly tempted to lewdness, and the demons themselves confessed the shameful lengths to which they had
gone, in vain, to defile their modesty.

It was thought expedient to turn to exorcisms. For that
purpose, Benedetto Merla, of the Order of Preachers, greatly
skilled in the cure of spiritual disorders, and Girolamo

Fontana, a priest, brother of the first three and uncle of the last, were sent for. But despite all their attempts, they could not find out whether the women were really moved by the Devil or by themselves. . . .

St. Ignatius Enters the Fray

One day while they were trying to find this out, Girolamo Bondinari, who was also the women's confessor, came into the room. Without their noticing what he did, he hung up a picture of St. Ignatius. The demons now revealed themselves as the horrible tormentors of the women's bodies, with dreadful cries, asking Bondinari why he had brought their cruel persecutor there.

Then they turned upon the saint with abusive words. They encouraged each other, saying that they would never yield to a bald-headed, limping old man who was half-blind, referring contemptuously to the saint. Nevertheless, one of the demons, who was the chief of the band, could not keep from fleeing away, leaving the woman on the ground, half-dead. When she came to herself, she said that she had seen a vision of St. Ignatius, who had encouraged her and promised her deliverance.

After this event, the demons showed themselves by obvious signs. They spoke in various tongues that the women had never known. They related things that were then happening in distant countries and predicted other things that later took place.

They walked on all fours with their knees fastened together. They knew and recognized the presence of hidden relics. Various parts of their bodies suddenly swelled, and the swelling just as quickly subsided, with other strange phenomena.

They were taken to the church of Our Lady of Reggio, to St. Agatha of Sorbara, and to St. Geminiano, all famous for the liberation of demoniacs. But all this was to no avail—for the glory of the act had been reserved by God for

St. Ignatius. The women, who understood this from what they had witnessed before, placed all their hope in him and vowed that they would keep his feast and fast on his vigil if they were delivered.

Meanwhile, a relic of the saint was brought from Rome. Even though it was secretly brought into the house, the demons immediately announced its presence, where it came from, and from whom. They said that he who could drive them out had now entered the house.

The same day, one of the fiercest of the unclean spirits, who had boasted that he would not budge a step for Ignatius, suddenly began to tremble. He exclaimed, "Ah, but it's not so; there goes forth a flame from his mouth that burns me! St. Ignatius, St. Ignatius drives me away!" Then he said that they would soon see other miracles of Ignatius, so that the demons themselves would be forced to cry out before the Pope—for Ignatius' canonization was coming soon. And then the demon departed from his victim.

"Ignatius Casts Me Out!"

After him, another of the chief demons, who had abused and mocked the saint and ridiculed his own companions who had fled, swore that he would stay where he was no matter what. He, too, was expelled. To cover the shame of his defeat, he threw himself on his knees before a thorn of Our Lord's crown and said, "I leave this body through the virtue of this thorn, but not because of Ignatius, who doesn't possess such power."

Then he uttered a horrible shriek and went on his knees before the image of the saint. He fell down with his mouth to the earth, saying, "Whether or not I want to, I'm forced to confess. It's Ignatius who casts me out!" Saying that, he went out of his victim.

Many others tried the same deceit, some saying that they yielded to one saint and some to another. But afterward, they all came and licked the ground beneath the image of

Ignatius and confessed that it was by his force that they were sent back to hell. There was one who cried out in a rage, "O Lucifer, where is your power? Here you are destroyed by a piece of paper with the picture of this priest on it, and you have no force to resist!"

Just as the picture and relics of the saint had such power over the evil spirits, so they were also driven away when the possessed person was given his autobiography to read. No sooner was a word uttered than troops of them who possessed their tongues exclaimed they would rather leave than be exposed to that cursed book. Others fled and exclaimed, "Oh God, you have stripped us of our glory to give it to a lame, wrinkled old priest!"

Such were the strange events that accompanied the deliverance of these four women, until they were entirely free.[11]

*   *   *   *

A Calvinist Comes for Exorcism

An important part of Ignatius' mission while on earth had been to win back those who had left the Catholic Church to join the new schismatic groups. According to the following testimony in the canonization proceedings, he continued that work in heaven.

*   *   *   *

At Ostrog in Poland in 1627, a noble lady belonging to the sect of Calvin was delivered from satanic possession to the great glory of the Catholic faith. The evidence of her possession was unmistakable, for even though she knew no other than her native tongue, she replied to questions in any language she was addressed in. The Calvinists did not have the courage

---

[11] Mariani, 349–53.

to attempt to cure her, so they were constrained by necessity to put her into Catholic hands. They made their petition to the rector of the Jesuit college.

He first demanded to know whether they were entirely convinced that she was a demoniac. They answered yes.

The man who was most urgent in his entreaties was an extremely obstinate Calvinist. He used to say that he would sooner be a dog or a pig than a Papist. To him, the rector said, "Don't you consider our ceremonies superstitious and our exorcisms meaningless? Why then do you come to us? Is it faith or necessity that brings you? Send for your own ministers and your schismatic priests, and see what power they have over the Devil. Then come to us. For it's only fair that the trial should be considered as a proof of the reality of the two religions."

The Calvinists excused themselves, saying that their ministers did not possess the power to cast out demons. If the Catholics succeeded in doing so, they would think quite differently of the Roman faith.

After this, a visit was made by the Catholic authorities to the woman to see if she was really possessed, which they soon confirmed: As soon as the rector sprinkled her with holy water and touched her with a relic of St. Ignatius without her knowing it, she began to writhe and twist her body, saying that a bone of St. Ignatius tormented her.

As the rector was even more eager to heal the souls of the Calvinists than the body of the woman, he instructed them to bring the book of Calvin's *Institutes* or some other book containing their own dogmas and give it to the woman. This was accordingly done, and the Devil began to kiss and caress it with great marks of joy. The rector then took it and hid a picture of St. Ignatius between the pages; then he presented it to her again. The demon drew back, screaming with anger, and would not even touch it.

Being compelled to acknowledge what it was he feared, the unclean spirit answered, "The picture of St. Ignatius that you have placed there!"

The Calvinists were greatly confounded at this, and one of them said in anger, "You Papists have a good understanding with the Devil, so you can do whatever you want with him."

One of the Jesuit fathers then said, "Since this evidence doesn't satisfy you, let's try this. I'll pray to God that if yours is the true faith, the Devil may pass into my body and torment me, but if the Catholic faith is true, he may enter into you for one hour only. Will this satisfy you?"

Not one of them would consent, and all were silent. Then they earnestly begged the rector to assist the poor woman if he could. The rector promised and then went away.

The Woman Is Delivered

The rector ordered a three-day fast in the college and other penances, offering alms and many Masses. Then one of our brothers went to visit the possessed, and on seeing him, she flew into a passion. However, if a Calvinist presented himself, she called him her dear friend.

The following facts were revealed when the demon was made to speak. First, the demon confessed that the Jesuits at Ostrog were his most hated enemies and that he attempted by every means in his power to render them hated in the city and to work against the good they did. Second, he had once tried to burn down the college, but he had not been able to conceal the fire long enough to be successful.

Third, he tried to enter the rooms of the fathers with evil intentions, but he was repulsed by Mary and Ignatius. To prove this, he described to one of the fathers all the articles in his room and their arrangement, and he added that a certain candle he had prepared for the feast of Candlemas would not be broken because it was put near the crucifix.

As Mass was being said in our church for the liberation of the woman, the demon from time to time uttered horrible cries, saying, "Now they are raising the Most High!" The solemn exorcism was fixed for the feast of the Purification.

The Calvinists begged that it might take place privately in the house, but the faith was not to be defrauded of so remarkable a testimony to its power over the Devil. So the woman was brought into the church in the presence of a vast multitude. She was tightly bound and placed before Our Lady's and St. Ignatius' altar. She sent forth horrible and terrifying cries. Before beginning, the rector addressed the people and exhorted them to repentance. They wept and showed great emotion.

The demon was asked who he was and how he had entered there. After great resistance, he said that his name was Ruteno and that an old sorceress named Rutena had introduced him into that body by means of a thread with which a garland of flowers was bound. The woman now possessed had carelessly put it on her head, as is the custom in that country.

He was then forced to say who had most power to cast him out after God. After writhing about, gnashing his teeth in spite, and shrieking out, he answered, "Mary and Ignatius."

The exorcism continued for two hours before the image of the saint, with invocation of the Blessed Virgin. Then the demon snatched the woman out of the hands of those who held her, and throwing her on the earth, as if dead, he left her. In a little time, she came to herself, and being assisted to rise, she was led before the Blessed Sacrament, weeping. As everyone wept with her, right then and there, she solemnly renounced her errors and professed the Catholic faith.[12]

* * * *

These are only a few of the testimonies to the power of St. Ignatius as a soldier who continues even from heaven to battle the powers of darkness.

---

[12] Mariani, 356–60.

- CHAPTER 14 -

ST. TERESA OF ÁVILA
Guardian of the Interior Castle
(1515–1582)

*Guard your heart with all vigilance, for
from it flow the springs of life.*
Proverbs 4:23

S t. Ignatius established the Jesuits, we might say, as a spiritual "special forces" unit to launch out into hostile territory. But the Church in his day was in dire need of reform, and the spiritual battles fought within her were just as fierce and essential to the divine strategy for her ultimate victory. One of the soldiers commissioned for these daunting battles was Teresa of Ávila.[1]

Teresa Sanchez was born to a noble family in Spain in 1515, when Ignatius was still a teenager dreaming of glory on the battlefield. Her mother died young, and when the older sister who had cared for her left home to marry, Teresa was sent to an Augustinian monastery for her education.

She remained there a year and a half, with God's call to religious life beginning to make itself felt in her heart. But she

---

[1] The following account is adapted from the stories in St. Teresa of Ávila, *The Life of St. Teresa of Jesus, of the Order of Our Lady of Carmel*, trans. David Lewis, 3rd ed. (New York: Benziger, 1904).

resisted the call, and when she became ill, her father brought her home. While there, she began to wrestle more seriously with the matter. She later noted in her autobiography,

> The Devil put before me that I could not endure the trials of the religious life, because of the delicate way I had been raised. I defended myself against him by noting the trials that Christ endured, and that it was not much for me to suffer something for His sake; besides, He would help me to bear it. . . . I endured many temptations during these days.[2]

Finally, after a struggle of three months, Teresa yielded to her vocation, though she felt no natural inclination to religious life. When her father refused to let her go, she left by stealth one night and went to the local Carmelite monastery. The nuns received her but informed her father that she was with them. He gave up his opposition, and her life as a nun began.

God or Satan?

In time, Teresa was moving into the deep waters of contemplative prayer. Her experiences brought her great joy and sweetness, and she believed that they drew her closer to God. But she knew of several notorious nuns who had been deceived by Satan through mystical experiences, claiming to receive private revelations from God. She worried that she, too, might be deceived.

At last, she realized that she needed the help of a spiritual director. Yet she was reluctant to find one because she feared that she had not grown enough in holiness to merit one. After some hesitation, she realized that it was the Enemy who was keeping her back from her intention.

---

[2] *Life of St. Teresa*, 42.

"The Devil must lay much stress on this strategy when someone is just beginning a course of virtue," she later wrote. "I could not overcome my repugnance to the thought of spiritual counsel. Satan knows that the whole relief of the soul consists in conferring with the friends of God. So I put off setting a time when I would resolve to do this. I waited to grow better first."[3]

Teresa did eventually find a spiritual director—a series of them, in fact—and when she found the right one, he helped her considerably. But she later noted that incompetent spiritual directors, especially those who were too indulgent, were a great evil and had done her much harm.[4]

A Bewitched Priest

During this time, one of Teresa's confessors was a priest who was too closely associated with a woman for whom he had a deep romantic affection. The situation was publicly known and causing considerable scandal. When Teresa investigated the matter, she found that the woman was engaging in occult practices and using a diabolical love charm to bewitch him.

> I procured further information about the matter from members of his household. I learned more of his ruinous state, and saw that the poor man's fault was not so grave, because the wretched woman had made use of enchantments, by giving him a little idol made of copper, which she had begged him to wear around his neck for love of her. No one had sufficient influence with the priest to persuade him to throw it away.
>
> As to this matter of enchantments, I do not believe it with certainty to be true. But I will relate what I saw, by way of warning to men to be on their guard against women who will do things of this kind. . . . In exchange

---

[3] *Life of St. Teresa*, 132.
[4] *Life of St. Teresa*, 47.

for the gratification of their will, and of that affection which the Devil suggests, they will hesitate at nothing.[5]

What happened next seemed to confirm that the idol was in fact diabolically infested. Teresa reported:

> To do me a favor, the priest gave me that little copper idol, and I had it at once thrown into a river. When he had given it up, like a man roused from deep sleep, he began to consider all that he had done in those years. Then, frightened about himself, he lamented his bad moral state, and that woman came to be abhorrent in his eyes. . . . In short, he broke off all relations with her utterly, and he was never weary of giving God thanks for the light He had given him.[6]

A year later, the priest died, and Teresa was grateful that he had been freed of his bondage in time.

Guarding the Interior Castle

In the following years, Teresa grew in holiness and in spiritual discernment. Eventually, she founded a new Carmelite convent with a strict rule that gave birth to similar convents and brought considerable reform to the order. The Enemy's opposition to her work was at times severe; as is usual when reforms take place, many were comfortable with a more lax rule and felt threatened by the new movement.

To offer guidance to the sisters who looked to her for leadership, Teresa wrote several works that have become spiritual classics and led to her declaration by Pope Paul VI in 1970 as the first woman Doctor of the Church. Among these classics was *The Interior Castle*. It was inspired by the vision God gave her of "a most beautiful crystal globe like a castle" that was illuminated by Christ the King, who was enthroned

---

[5] *Life of St. Teresa*, 48.
[6] *Life of St. Teresa*, 48–49.

at the center of the fortress "in the greatest splendor. . . . But outside the castle all was darkness, with toads, vipers, and other poisonous vermin." [7]

Then, however, the vision took a disturbing turn. While Teresa was admiring the beauty that God gives to souls:

> The light suddenly disappeared and, although the King of Glory did not leave the castle, the crystal was covered with darkness and was left as ugly as coal and with an unbearable stench, and the poisonous creatures outside the wall were able to get into the castle. Such was the state of a soul in sin.[8]

In many ways, Teresa's personal mission was that of the soldier assigned to guard that interior castle—both her own and those of the women under her care—from the diabolical forces outside.

Wise Counsel

In her writings, Teresa provides wise counsel for souls who seek to become fully united with God. She refers often to Satan, warning about his wily strategies to keep us from prayer and other beneficial spiritual disciplines. For example, when speaking of false humility, she observed:

> But it is necessary that we should understand what kind of humility this should be, because Satan, I believe, does great harm. For he hinders those who begin to pray from going onward, by suggesting to them false notions of humility. He makes them think it is pride to have great spiritual desires, to wish to imitate the saints, and to long for martyrdom. He tells us right off, or he makes us

[7] *Biblioteca Mística Carmelitana*, ed. Silverio de Santa Teresa (Burgos: El Monte Carmelo, 1934), vol. 18, 276-78, quoted in *The Collected Works of St. Teresa of Ávila*, trans. Kieran Kavanaugh, O.C.D., and Otilio Rodriguez, O.C.D. (Washington, D.C.: ICS Publications, 1980), vol. 2, 268.

[8] *Collected Works*, 268-69.

think, that the actions of the saints are to be admired, not to be imitated, by us who are sinners.[9]

Satan often tempts souls to feel that because of their sins, it would be useless or even hypocritical to pray. She provides sound advice to those who are tempted this way:

> Let no one who has begun to give himself to prayer be discouraged, and say: "If I fall into sin, it will be worse for me if I go on now with the practice of prayer." I think that's true if he gives up prayer, and doesn't correct his evil ways. But if he doesn't give up prayer, let him be assured of this: Prayer will bring him to the haven of light.
>
> In this matter the Devil turned his big artillery on me, and I suffered so much because I thought it showed a lack of humility if I persevered in prayer when I was so wicked. So I gave up praying for at least a year. But doing this was only throwing myself down into hell, nor could it have been otherwise. There was no need for any demons to drag me there.
>
> O my God, was there ever blindness so great as this? How well Satan prepares his measures for his purpose, when he pursues us in this way! The traitor knows that he has already lost the soul that perseveres in prayer, and that every fall he can bring about only helps such a soul, by the goodness of God, to make greater progress in His service. No wonder Satan is so eager to stop that soul from praying![10]

With regard to bodily disciplines, Teresa noted, the Devil tries to dismay us by fears for our health.

> When Satan sees us a little anxious about practicing spiritual disciplines, he works to keep us from them. He wants nothing more than to convince us that our way of life

---

[9] *Life of St. Teresa*, 81.

[10] *Life of St. Teresa*, 145–46.

will certainly kill us and destroy our health. Even tears of remorse, he suggests, will make us blind! I went through this, so I know all about it. But I know of no better sight or better health that we can desire than the loss of both for such a good cause. . . .

When it pleased God to let me discover this strategy of Satan, who suggested to me that I was ruining my health, I used to say to the Enemy that my death was of no consequence. When he suggested rest, I replied that I did not want rest, but the Cross.[11]

The fears for our health, Teresa concluded, are greatly exaggerated. But if we determine to serve God despite those fears, the Enemy loses his power to thwart our progress.

More Devilish Strategies

Yet another way the Devil tempts those who are growing in holiness, Teresa warns, is through provoking us to be upset over the sins of others.

There is another temptation—we ought to be aware of it, and be cautious in our conduct: Persons are carried away by a zeal for virtue, through the pain they feel at the sight of the sins and failings of others. Satan tells them that this pain arises only out of their desire that God may not be offended, and out of their anxiety about His honor. So they immediately seek to remedy the evil. This so disturbs them, so that they cannot pray.

The greatest evil of all lies in their thinking that this is an act of virtue, of perfection, and of a great zeal for God. . . . So the soul that wants to apply itself to prayer finds its security in casting away from itself all anxiety about persons and things, in taking care of itself, and in pleasing God. This is the most profitable course.[12]

---

[11] *Life of St. Teresa*, 82.
[12] *Life of St. Teresa*, 82–83, 221–22.

Teresa notes that this is not the case with public sins, heresies, or attacks on the Church. Because they lead people to
stumble or go astray, we must be concerned about them. But
in private matters, we must not let the sins of others disturb
us so much that they hinder our prayers. If we do, the Devil
has won a battle.

The saint offers a sober warning, even to those who are
more advanced in prayer:

> A soul may reach the stage where it receives great graces
> from God in prayer. But it must never rely on itself,
> because it may fall. Nor should it expose itself in any way
> whatever to any risks of sin. This principle should be well
> considered because so much depends on it. For here is
> the delusion that Satan can create in order to entangle
> us afterward: Though the grace truly is from God, the
> traitor will make use of that very grace, as far as he can,
> for his own purposes.[13]

And the trap he lays on this occasion, no doubt, is spiritual pride.

In all these matters, Teresa learned from hard experience just how effective the Enemy's strategies can be. "What
difficulties and what terrors Satan employs," she lamented,
"against those who want to draw close to God!"[14]

Extraordinary Demonic Activity

Temptation in all its various forms is what the Church has
traditionally called the ordinary activity of the Devil. But
as is apparent in the lives of earlier saints, extraordinary
forms of activity appear as well, which typically occur in cases
of the demonic infestation of objects or buildings or the possession of human victims. Teresa's experience in spiritual

---

[13] *Life of St. Teresa*, 111–112.
[14] *Life of St. Teresa*, 136.

combat was by no means limited to the ordinary forms of the Enemy's activity. She tells several stories in her autobiography, as adapted in the following accounts.[15]

*   *   *   *

Now that I have described certain temptations and troubles, interior and secret, of which Satan was the cause, I will speak of others that he practically worked in public and in which his presence could not be ignored.

I was once in an oratory when Satan, in an abominable shape, appeared at my left hand. I looked at his mouth in particular, because he spoke, and it was horrible. A huge flame seemed to issue out of his body, perfectly bright, without any shadow. He spoke in a fearful way, telling me that, though I had escaped out of his hands, he would yet lay hold of me again.

I was in great terror, making the Sign of the Cross as well as I could, and then the form vanished—but it reappeared instantly. This occurred twice. I did not know what to do. There was some holy water at hand; I took some and threw it in the direction of the figure, and then Satan never returned.

On another occasion, I was tortured for five hours with such terrible pains, both interior and bodily sufferings, that it seemed to me as if I could not bear them any longer. Those who were with me were frightened. They had no idea what to do, and I could not help myself.

When such pains and bodily ailments become unbearable, it is my habit to make, as well as I can, interior acts of petition to Our Lord. I beg Him, if His Majesty can be served by doing so, to give me the patience to endure it, even to the end of the world. So when I found myself suffering so cruelly, I found some relief in making those interior resolutions, so that I might be able to endure the pain.

---

[15] The following narrative is adapted from *Life of St. Teresa*, 173–76.

It pleased Our Lord to let me understand that this was
the work of Satan, because I saw close beside me a most
frightful, black little creature, gnashing his teeth in despair
at losing what he attempted to seize. When I saw him, I
laughed and had no fear.

Those sisters who were with me were unable to assist me,
and they knew of no remedy for relieving such great pain.
My body, head, and arms were violently shaken; I could
not help myself. But worst of all was the interior pain, for
I couldn't find peace of any kind. I didn't dare ask for holy
water, because it might frighten the sisters to find out what
was actually happening.

The Devils Flee From Holy Water

I know by frequent experience that nothing puts the demons
to flight like holy water. They run away from the Sign of the
Cross as well, but they return immediately. So the power of
holy water must be great indeed.

As for me, my soul is conscious of a special and most dis-
tinctive consolation whenever I use it. In fact, I almost always
feel a certain refreshing that I cannot describe, together with
an inward joy that comforts my whole soul. This is no mere
imagination, nor something that has occurred only once. It
has happened very often, and I have observed it very carefully.

I compare this relief I feel to what happens when a
person who is quite hot and thirsty drinks a cup of cold
water. His whole being is refreshed. I consider that everything ordained by the Church is very important, and I find
joy in seeing that the words of the Church are so mighty
they can actually endow water with power, so that there is a
great difference between holy water and water that has never
been blessed.

Since my pains didn't cease, I said to my friends, "If you
won't laugh, I'll ask for some holy water." They brought me
some and sprinkled me with it, but I felt no better.

Then I myself threw some on the demon. Immediately he went away. All my sufferings ended, just as if someone had taken them by hand from me. But I was exhausted, as if I'd been beaten with many blows.

It was of great service to me to learn this: If, by Our Lord's permission, Satan can do so much evil to a soul and body not in his power, how much more can he do when he has them in his possession? It gave me a renewed desire to be delivered from such dangerous company.

Another time, and not long ago, the same thing happened to me, though it didn't last as long, and I was alone at the moment. I asked for holy water, and those who came in after the demon had gone away—they were two nuns, worthy of all credit, and would not under any circumstances tell a lie—smelled a most offensive odor, like that of burning sulfur. I smelled nothing myself, but the odor lingered long enough for them to smell it.

On another occasion, I was in the choir when, in a moment, I became profoundly recollected in prayer. I went out so that the sisters might know nothing of it. Yet those who were near heard the sound of heavy blows where I was, and I heard voices myself, as of persons in consultation. I didn't hear what they said; I was so absorbed in prayer that I understood nothing, and I wasn't at all afraid of them. This took place almost always when Our Lord was pleased to allow me to persuade someone to advance in the spiritual life. . . .

Don't Fear the Demons

One night I thought the evil spirits were about to suffocate me. But when the sisters threw holy water around me, I saw a great troop of them rush away as if tumbling over a precipice. These cursed spirits have tormented me so often, but now I'm hardly afraid of them, because I realize that they cannot even move without Our Lord's permission. . . .

I hope that what I have written will be of use to the true servant of God, who should pay no attention to these terrors, which Satan sends only to make him afraid! Let him understand that each time we dismiss these terrors, their force is lessened, and the soul gains power over them. There is always some great good obtained. . . .

Freeing Souls From Purgatory

Once on the night of All Souls, I was in an oratory. After reciting one nocturn, I was saying some very devotional prayers at the end of our breviary, when Satan put himself on the book before me to prevent my finishing my prayer. I made the Sign of the Cross, and he went away.

I then returned to my prayer, and he too came back. He did this, I believe, three times, and I wasn't able to finish the prayer without throwing holy water at him. When I did, I saw at that moment certain souls come out of purgatory. They must have been near the point of their deliverance; perhaps Satan, I thought, might in this way have been trying to delay their release by hindering my prayer. . . .

Angels Fighting Demons

I wish to tell the following because I was greatly disturbed by it. On Trinity Sunday, in the choir of a certain monastery, while I was in rapture, I saw a great fight between evil spirits and the angels.

I couldn't make out what the vision meant. But within two weeks, it was explained clearly enough by the dispute that took place between persons given to prayer and many who were not. The dispute did great harm to that community because it was a dispute that lasted a long time and caused much trouble.

On another occasion, I saw a great host of evil spirits all around me. At the same time, I saw a great light that surrounded me and kept them from coming near me. I understood it to mean that God was watching over me, so that they might not approach me and try to make me offend Him.

I knew the vision was real by what I saw occasionally within myself. The fact is, I know now how little power the evil spirits have, provided I'm not out of the grace of God. I have hardly any fear of them at all, for their power is nothing if they don't find the souls they assault to be cowards who give up the fight. But with such souls, they show their power.

Now and then, during the temptations I'm speaking of, it seemed to me as if all my vanity and weakness in times past had become alive again within me. So I had good reason to commit myself into the hands of God. Then I was tormented by the thought that because these things came back to my memory, I must be utterly in the power of Satan. I had imagined that even the first stirring of an evil thought shouldn't come near someone who had received from Our Lord such great graces as I had. But my confessor put my mind at ease. . . .

A Demon-Oppressed Priest

Once when I was going to Communion, I saw with the eyes of the soul, more distinctly than with those of the body, two demons of most hideous shape. Their horns seemed to encompass the throat of the poor priest. I beheld my Lord, in that great majesty of which I have spoken, held in the hands of that priest, in the Host he was about to give me.

It was plain that the hands were those of a sinner, and I felt that the soul of that priest was in mortal sin. What must it be, O my Lord, to look upon Your beauty amid shapes so hideous! The two demons were so frightened and intimidated in Your presence that they seemed as if they would have willingly run away, had You but given them permission.

I was so troubled by the vision that I don't know how I was able to receive Communion. I was also in great fear, for

I thought that if the vision was truly from God, then His Majesty wouldn't have allowed me to see the evil state of that soul.

Our Lord Himself told me to pray for that priest. He said He had allowed this vision so I might understand the power of the words of consecration and how God didn't fail to be truly present in the Host, no matter how wicked the priest might be who uttered those words. He also wanted me to see His great goodness in that He places Himself in the very hands of His enemy, for my good and for the good of all.

I understood clearly how the priests are under greater obligation to be holy than other persons and what a horrible thing it is to receive this most Holy Sacrament unworthily; how great is the Devil's dominion over a soul in mortal sin. It did me a great service and made me fully understand what I owe to God. May He be blessed forevermore!

*   *   *   *

The Victor's Crown

Teresa's spiritual combat concluded with her death in 1582. As she prepared herself for the end, she sang joyfully, despite considerable pain. "Now the hour has come for me to leave this exile," she prayed, "and my soul rejoices at one with You, for what I have so desired!"

As she was leaving this earthly battlefield, the sisters in the room and nearby reported visions of angels and saints taking her home to be at last with "His Majesty," her Commander and Spouse. In a vision years before, He had promised her a crown. Almost immediately after her death, miracles began to occur, confirming that Teresa had indeed received at last, after so many battles, that victor's crown.[16]

---

[16] William Thomas Walsh, St. Teresa of Ávila: A Biography (repr., Rockford, Ill.: TAN Books, 1987), 579–82.

- CHAPTER 15 -

ST. MARTIN DE PORRES
Humble Foot Soldier
(1579–1639)

Do not be overcome by evil, but overcome evil with good.
Romans 12:21

With the exploration and colonization of the Americas by Europeans in the sixteenth and seventeenth centuries, the ancient spiritual war opened up new fields of battle. Demonic powers plaguing the Old World joined forces with those of the New. The result was carnage, cruelty, exploitation, and slavery.

Yet the conquerors, driven so often by pride, vainglory, and lust for gold and power, did not arrive alone on the new shores. Missionaries bringing the gospel came as well. A new light was shining in the darkness.

As it turned out, their mission was not just to bring light to peoples who had never heard the name of Jesus Christ. They had to fight as well the demons who provoked their own countrymen to arrogant attitudes and acts of gross injustice. And even they themselves often succumbed to the Enemy's temptation to pride and severity in dealing with the native peoples.

The ancient land of Peru, on the western coast of the South American continent, suffered more than its share of misery. In 1532, the emperor of the Incas had only recently defeated and executed his half-brother in a civil war when he himself was defeated and executed by the Spaniard conquistador Francisco Pizarro. In 1535, the conqueror founded at Lima a new capital city for a new colony.[1]

The first years of Lima's history were troubled by Satan's provocations to covet wealth and power. The Spaniards committed atrocities against the natives in their demands for treasure, and they fought one another for posts of honor and profit. The city had not yet celebrated the seventh anniversary of its founding when Pizarro was murdered in his palace by one of his own men.

Martin and the Dominicans

Dominican missionaries were the first to preach in Peru, having come to the land with Pizarro. Other religious orders sent missionaries there as well, but the Dominican influence was dominant. The first bishop of Lima was a Dominican, as was the first center of Christian culture, the University of St. Mark.

In 1594, the Dominican brothers at the Holy Rosary Convent in Lima opened their doors to a humble, unassuming young teenager named Martin. His father was John de Porres, a noble Spanish gentleman and a knight of the Order of Alcántara. Martin's mother was John's mistress, Anna Velázquez, a freed slave from Panama, of African and perhaps part Native American descent. Though at first John had refused to recognize Martin as his son, eventually he repented of that injustice.

Martin had been apprenticed to a barber at the age of twelve. In those days, barbers did much more than cut hair and trim beards. They commonly served as doctors,

---

[1] This account of St. Martin's life is based largely on the narrative in Giuliana Cavalini, *St. Martin de Porres: Apostle of Charity*, trans. Caroline Holland (repr., Charlotte, N.C.: TAN Books, 2010).

pharmacists, and even surgeons. Martin had learned the craft well and seemed to have a special gift for healing.

Now the young man brought his gift and skills to the monastery to seek admission as a Third Order *donado*, or lay helper. It was the most humble post there, ranking even below the lay brothers. *Donados* took on the lowliest and hardest tasks in the community—toilet cleaning included—in exchange for food, lodging, and a simple habit.

Before long, Martin's humility, compassion, and deep devotion to God were evident not just to the brothers but to people throughout Lima. The poor turned to him for material assistance; people of every class sought him out for medical care and counsel. He often left the monastery walls to care for those in need across the city.

Meanwhile, Martin began to demonstrate extraordinary gifts of the Holy Spirit: instantaneous cures and other miracles; levitation, bilocation, and aerial flight; prophecy and other forms of preternatural knowledge; invisibility; and the ability to communicate with animals. But as usual, where the power of God was manifest, the Enemy's pride compelled him to display his malicious handiwork.

A Demon on the Stairway

Martin's patient humility was obvious to all who met him. Yet the brothers sometimes took advantage of his mild and accommodating spirit, and many citizens of the city looked down on him because of his mixed racial heritage. Nevertheless, he always returned good for any evil that was done to him.

The one exception to Martin's habit of mildness was his dealing with the Devil. When he encountered the Enemy face to face, he was stern and commanding, confident of the authority that his spiritual Commander had given him. His strategy to resist Satan was simple but effective.

One night Martin left his cell to visit a patient in the infirmary. He was loaded down with medical supplies and a brazier filled with burning coals. He made his way carefully to an old stairway in the monastery, tucked away in a dark corner and in disrepair. It had been closed off as a safety hazard, but he wanted to take it because it was the shortest path between his cell and the infirmary.

When he reached the stairway, he was confronted by the horrible sight of a monster barring his way. From the hideous figure emerged a frightening caricature of a human face. The eyes were flashing with malice and rage, and Martin knew it was the Devil.

"What are you doing here, you accursed one?" Martin demanded.

"I'm here because it pleases me to be here," came the curt reply.

"Away with you, then," said Martin, "to the cursed depths where you dwell!"

The beast would not budge, and Martin realized that any further conversation would be fruitless. So he set down the brazier and the medical supplies, took off his leather belt, and began whipping the Demon with it.

The evil spirit vanished—not because of the blows from the belt, of course, since spirits have no material bodies of their own, but because apparently the Devil realized that he was wasting his time trying to get in Martin's way.

The young man next took a firebrand from the brazier, drew the Sign of the Cross on the wall where the Demon had appeared, and knelt to pray. He thanked God for giving him the victory over his Enemy.

The Devil Comes to Martin's Cell

One day in a gathering of Dominican novices and professed brothers, one of the priests of the Holy Rosary friary reported, "Last night Martin had a dreadful battle with the

demon and conquered him." This time, the Devil had not
been waiting for him on the stairs, but instead came to Martin's room.[2]

But Martin was not alone. Francis de la Torre, the offi-
cer of the guard, had been sharing Martin's room for several months. Some years later, he recalled what he had seen
that night.

Francis slept in the back of the room, separated from
the front by an alcove. Just as he was about to retire for the
night, he heard the door open and close. When he heard
the normally mild and patient Martin speak to the visitor in
anger, he knew something was wrong.

"Why have you come here, you troublemaker? What are
you looking for? This is not your room. Get out!"

The demon refused to leave. Perhaps it was a legion of
demons, as in the Gospel story, because Martin's words were
followed by a hellish commotion. Then Martin was seized
and brutally beaten.

Francis wanted to know why there was such an uproar,
so he stuck his head out of the alcove to see. He saw Martin being mercilessly rolled back and forth on the floor and
thrown against the walls. He watched as Martin flinched and
moaned under the diabolical assault. The commotion continued, yet he could see no one in the cell but Martin.

Suddenly the room and some of its furnishings burst
into flames. Francis leapt into action to extinguish the blaze,
and he and Martin finally put it out. Then suddenly the
clamor ended, and all was calm again.

Francis returned to his bed in the alcove. Martin lay
down on the wooden plank that served for his bed with the
stone that served as the pillow under his head. Both men fell
asleep, tired but at peace.

At three in the morning, Martin rose to ring the dawn
bell and light a candle for his companion. Francis jumped

---

[2] Cavalini, 40–42.

out of bed to see how much damage the fire had done. He was amazed to find that the walls, the furniture, and the linens arranged on the shelves showed not even a trace of the fire or the smoke. Yet Francis himself had seen them all in flames only a few hours before!

Martin had indeed conquered the Demon.

A Final Assault

Nine years after his admission to the monastery as a lay helper, Martin finally made his profession as a lay brother. He spent the rest of his life passionately devoted to Our Lord and His people. Martin's life demonstrated a remarkable balance of prayer and action: His hours were spent both in joyful contemplation and in tireless corporal works of mercy, caring for the poor, the sick, widows, and orphans.

In 1639, Martin went to bed one day with a raging fever. He knew his time on earth was drawing to a close, and word had spread around the city that the holy man was dying. So the Devil sought one last chance to harass him.

As the old man lay in bed, the Enemy came close and whispered, trying to tempt him to pride in his final hour. "Now you've won!" he said. "You've spurned all obstacles beneath your feet. You're a saint! You can stop beating your breast; now is the moment of triumph!"

The brothers around Martin's bed could see on his face that he was struggling inside with these thoughts. They watched and prayed for his victory, waiting to see the outcome. Then one of the friars said, "Brother Martin, don't argue with the Demon! He can make white seem black and black seem white with his deceitful arguments and quibbling."

Martin opened his eyes and managed an impish smile. "Have no fear that the Demon will waste his arguments on anyone who isn't a theologian," he said, with his usual modesty. "He's too proud to use them against a poor black man!"

He died soon after, and the ancient Enemy lost yet another battle for a magnificent soul. Martin's great humility served him to the very end as his impenetrable armor against the Devil's wiles. And his unflagging compassion had driven back the Enemy's darkness all across a city that was in desperate need of the Light.

- CHAPTER 16 -

ST. JOHN VIANNEY
Field Hospital Medic
(1786–1859)

*Resist the Devil and he will flee from you. . . . Cleanse
your hands, you sinners, and purify your hearts, you men
of double mind. . . . Confess your sins to one another,
and pray for one another, that you may be healed.*
James 4:7, 8; 5:16

The intellectual movement now called the Enlightenment
no doubt brought illumination to some aspects of life
in the Western world throughout the eighteenth century.
Science became more rigorous in its methods. Political philosophers opened up new horizons that ultimately led to the
establishment of the American republic and a more vigorous
notion of political liberty.

But the Enlightenment had its terrifying shadows as
well. With roots, some have argued, in Martin Luther's
revolt against the Church's authority, many of the leaders
of the Enlightenment movement saw the Catholic Church
as the enemy of reason and progress. The bitter fruit of that
animosity was evident most clearly in France. There, the
Revolution of 1789 to 1799, overthrowing the monarchy, led
to the brutal oppression of faithful Catholics.[1]

---

[1] See, for example, Bertrand Russell, *A History of Western Philosophy: And Its
Connection With Political and Social Circumstances From the Earliest Times to the
Present Day* (New York: Simon & Schuster, 1945), 492–94.

During the aptly named Reign of Terror in 1793 and 1794, the Devil used the revolutionaries and the mobs they stirred up as his pawns to assault the Church. Priests and religious leaders were imprisoned and massacred; churches and other Catholic properties throughout the nation were either confiscated or destroyed. An attempt was even made to establish a "Cult of Reason" to replace the Catholic faith altogether, with its own rites and festivals eclipsing religious ones.

Counter-rebellions emerged throughout France. Faithful Catholics hid priests from the authorities, resisted the activity of revolutionary agents, and in some cases, even took up arms. But it was not until 1801, after Napoleon rose to power, that the French government once again made its peace, however uneasy, with the Church.

An Unlikely Candidate for the Priesthood

It was in fact a young soldier in Napoleon's army who was to become the most famous spiritual warrior of post-Revolutionary France. John Vianney had been born during the Revolution and raised in a devout Catholic family of farmers that had traveled to distant farms in order to celebrate Masses in secret. He grew up admiring priests as spiritual war heroes because they risked their lives to minister to the people.

Not surprisingly, then, at the age of twenty, John enrolled in a school to be trained for Holy Orders. But he struggled with his studies, especially Latin. In 1809, he was drafted for the army, even though ecclesiastical students in most areas of the country were exempt from the draft. Unable to put his heart into Napoleon's ill-advised wars, he deserted and hid from the authorities until the emperor issued an amnesty for deserters.

John resumed his studies, yet he continued to struggle. His teachers had serious doubts about his intellectual competence to become a priest. But at last he was ordained and eventually appointed as the parish priest in a little village named Ars, a town of about 230 residents. He spent the rest of his life there.

Field Hospital Medic

The ancient Enemy had made sure that the Enlightenment and the bloody Revolution took their toll on the faith of the people. Such a prolonged and furious assault on the Church had contributed to widespread religious ignorance and indifference. Even in the rural area where John was ministering, far from the notorious temptations of life in the big city, the Devil was busy.

John's counterattack employed two primary strategies: preaching and hearing confessions. His hard-hitting sermons offended many. But he refused to back down from his condemnations of pride and hypocrisy, laziness and materialism, impurity and drunkenness, and even gossip.[2]

Despite considerable human opposition and the Devil's attempts to harden hearts, many were converted by John's preaching. As a result, the confessional at Ars became a field hospital for those who had been wounded on the spiritual battlefield. Eventually, John's reputation as a confessor and spiritual director spread beyond Ars, and people came from far away to receive his counsel. So great was his fortitude that he often spent sixteen to eighteen hours a day hearing confessions.

Given these spiritual victories, and the true Light that beamed from Ars out into the darkness, Satan was sure to retaliate. But few could have expected the ferocity of the preternatural assaults that came. The following accounts come from a memoir written by one of his contemporaries.[3]

---

[2] See St. Jeanne-Baptiste Marie Vianney, *The Sermons of the Curé of Ars*, trans. Una Morrissy (repr., Charlotte, N.C.: TAN Books, 1995).

[3] The following sections are adapted from various accounts in Georgina Molyneux, *The Curé D'Ars: A Memoir of Jean-Baptiste Marie Vianney*, 2nd ed. (London: Richard Bentley, 1869), 138–57.

* * * *

The Disturbances Begin

Soon after John opened an orphanage in the village, strange noises began to disturb his rest at night. He later reported:

"About nine o'clock at night I was just going to bed when the demon came to torment me for the first time. Three heavy blows were struck on the door of my courtyard, as if someone were trying to force it open. I opened my window and asked, 'Who's there?' But I saw nothing, so I commended myself to God and quietly retired.

"But before I'd gone to sleep, I was startled again by three knocks that were louder still—not now on the outer door, but on the one at the staircase that led to my bedroom. I got up and cried out a second time, 'Who's there?' No one answered.

"When these noises at night first began, I thought they were caused by burglars, so I thought I'd better take some precautions. I asked two brave men to sleep in the house who were ready to help me if I needed them. They came several nights in a row.

"They heard the noise but found nothing. So they were convinced that it had some causes other than the malice of men. I myself soon came to the same conclusion.

"One night in the middle of winter, I heard three violent knocks. I got up quickly from my bed and went down into the courtyard, expecting to see the intruders making their escape, and intending to call for help. But to my astonishment, I saw nothing, I heard nothing, and even more, I found no traces of footprints in the snow. So I resigned myself to God's will, asking Him to be my guard and protector and to surround me with His angels if my Enemy should return again to torment me."

Others Hear the Noises

In these early days of the demonic activity, which went on every night for hours, the saint was frightened. He later recalled that many times he was ready to die in his bed with fear. Under the strain, his health declined.

Finally some friends offered to keep guard around the rectory and sleep in the adjoining room. Several armed young men stationed themselves near the church, where they could observe anyone who approached the building. The attacks continued.

Some of these good people were quite terrified, including the wheelwright of the village. When it came his turn to act as sentinel, he took up a position in a room in the rectory with his gun by his side. At midnight, he heard a frightful crash close to him.

It seemed to him that all the furniture in the room was smashed to pieces under a storm of invisible blows. The poor man cried out for help, and the curé came quickly to his assistance. They searched the room and the rest of the house, examining every corner, but all in vain.

When John was convinced that the sounds had no human origin, he dismissed his guards. Little by little, his fear was diminished, and in the end, he became somewhat accustomed to these astonishing events.

Fears of Damnation

Before this period, poor John had been prey to a different kind of conflict. He had been tormented by the most despairing thoughts of his future destiny. He seemed continually to see under his feet the lake of fire and to hear a voice telling him that his place was already marked in it.

Day and night, John was haunted by the fear of being eternally lost. But after having combated and overcome this internal temptation, he had less difficulty in resisting his external, though invisible, foes. Still, the oppression to

which he was now subjected was no light one. It lasted not
for days or months but for thirty-five years, with different
phases and under different forms, but almost without even
temporary relief.

John became so familiar with the demon who tormented
him that he even gave him a nickname: the *grappin* ("wrestler"). "Oh, the *grappin* and myself?" he once joked. "We are
almost buddies!"

"You Truffle-Eater!"

Often, at midnight, three violent knocks on the door alerted
the curé that his enemy was present. These knocks were followed by others—louder if he were sleeping more soundly,
softer if he were sleeping more lightly. The demon would
entertain himself by making a terrible uproar on the staircase, then enter the room and seize the bed curtains, shaking them violently. The poor priest never could understand
why they failed to be torn to shreds.

Sometimes the evil spirit knocked as if he were demand-
ing admittance. Then the next moment, though the door
remained shut, he was in the room, rearranging the furniture,
and rummaging around everywhere. He called out to the
priest with a mocking voice, "Vianney! Vianney!" and would
add to his name the most outrageous labels and threats.
"You truffle-eater, we'll get you! We have a hold on you!"

At other times, the demon called to John from the
courtyard. After shouting for a long time, he would imitate
a charge of cavalry or the sound of a marching army. Sometimes he drove nails into the floor as if with a hammer,
sometimes he cut wood, sometimes he sawed and planed
planks. He sounded like a carpenter busily occupied with
remodeling the interior of the house. At other times, he
drummed on the table, the chimney, or the water jug,
always choosing objects that would make the loudest noise.

More Extraordinary Phenomena

Sometimes a noise came from the hall below like a horse bounding up to the ceiling and then falling down heavily on his four feet. At other times, it was the bleating of a flock of sheep grazing over his head.

One night when John was disturbed more than usual, he said, "My God, I willingly make to You the sacrifice of a few hours' sleep for the conversion of sinners." Immediately, the demons vanished, and everything fell silent.

For several consecutive nights, he heard such loud and menacing clamors in the courtyard that he trembled with fear. These voices spoke in an unknown tongue and in the most confused way. The tumult they made recalled to John's mind the recent military invasion of the country; he compared it to the noise of an Austrian army. And on another occasion, making a comparison even more characteristic of him, he said, "Troops of demons held their parliament in my courtyard."

One night a demon sang in his chimney like a nightingale. At other times, the demons pulled him out of bed. One morning, his discipline (a cord made for self-mortification) suddenly rose up off the table by itself and began slithering along like a snake. A rope was fastened to one end of it, and when the priest grabbed it, it was stiff like wood. When he set it back on the table, it began to slither again, going around three times.

On another night, he was suddenly awakened by feeling himself lifted up in the air. "But I armed myself with the Sign of the Cross," John recalled, "and the *grappin* left me."

Cunning But Not Strong

John was not the only one to witness these startling manifestations, which became increasingly bizarre. They followed him to other places—on the road, in his lodgings, once even in a confessional. He was lifted up in the air; he was pulled around in his bed. The demons shrieked and moaned under his bed, and once they even set his bed on fire.

One night, after an especially violent assault, John rose from bed to answer the doorbell. There he found a man who had traveled some miles to make his confession. Actually, this was not an unusual occurrence; often, after the worst nights, the priest found at his door in the morning several pilgrims who had made long journeys to have him hear their confessions. In fact, whenever the persecution was more fierce than usual, he took it as a sign of some special mercy or consolation about to be granted to him.

The saint took it all in stride and learned how to deal with his tormentors. "The demon is very cunning," he once observed, "but he is not strong. Making a Sign of the Cross soon puts him to flight. A few days ago he made an uproar, like the sound of all the carriages in Lyons driving over my head. Only last night, whole troops of demons were shaking my door and babbling like an army of Austrians. I didn't understand a word they said. But when I made the Sign of the Cross, they departed."

Skeptical Brother Priests

John's brother priests were at first little inclined to believe in the reality of these diabolical manifestations. They sought to account for them by natural physiological causes. "If the Curé d'Ars lived like other men," they insisted, "if he took a proper quantity of sleep and nourishment, his imagination would be calmed, his brain would no longer be peopled with specters, and all these hellish hallucinations would vanish."

Now there was a respectable curé who had known and loved John since the beginning of his ministry at Ars. He was eager to procure for his people the benefit of John's presence among them, so he begged him to join the missionaries who were about to celebrate the approaching jubilee with the usual services. John immediately agreed. He remained three weeks at Saint-Trivier, preached from time to time, and served as confessor for many penitents.

By this time, the harassment to which John was subjected by his spiritual foes was talked about everywhere. His clerical companions made it a subject of amusement. "Come, come, dear curé," they said. "Do as others do. Nourish yourself better. That's the way to end all their antics."

One night, however, they assumed a more serious tone. The discussion became more animated, and the banter of John's companions more bitter and reproachful. It was agreed that all this diabolical mystical experience was the result of delirium and hallucination. As a result, the poor priest was treated as a false visionary and an enthusiast.

To all this, he answered not a word but instead retired to his room. Apparently, all he could feel was joy over being persecuted. Soon afterwards, his joking companions went to their separate rooms for the night. They had the apathy of so-called wise men who, if they believed in the existence of the Devil at all, had only a feeble confidence that he would intervene in the affairs of the Curé d'Ars.

The Skeptics Are Convinced

Nevertheless, at midnight, all the guests in the house were awakened by a horrible brawl. The building was shaken from the very foundation, the doors banged, the windows clattered, the walls tottered, and sinister sounds of cracking were heard, as if the whole edifice were just about to fall to the ground.

In a moment, everyone was on his feet. They remembered that before he went to bed, John had said, "Don't be surprised if you hear a noise tonight." So they all rushed into his room, where they found him peacefully at rest.

"Get up!" they shouted. "The house is falling down!"

"Yes, I know what it is," he replied, smiling. "Go back to sleep; there's nothing to fear." They were reassured, and the noise stopped.

An hour later, a faint bell was heard. John got up and went to the door, where he found a man who had traveled several miles to confess to him. This, as we have noted, was no unusual occurrence. It often happened that after the cruelest nights, the curé found at his door in the morning pilgrims who had made long journeys in order to make their confessions to him.

Indeed, when the persecution he suffered was more violent than usual, he received it as a sign of some notable mercy or some special consolation about to be granted to him. One of the missionaries who experienced that evening's diabolical events was so impressed with the strange adventure we have just recounted that, when relating it afterward, he said, "I have made a vow to God never again to joke over these histories of apparitions and nocturnal noises. As for the Curé d'Ars, I believe him to be a saint."

In the meantime, John's tormentor appeared to be unceasingly occupied in devising new modes of attack. No longer content with disturbing his unfortunate victim by frightful noises and knocking on doors, he now sometimes hid under his bed. All night long, the poor curé's rest was interrupted and his thoughts distracted by piercing cries, mournful groans, or smothered sighs.

An Exorcism Using Relics

John was also called upon at times to deliver the possessed from their torment. The priest carried around with him a reliquary, with relics of Our Lord's passion and of some of the saints, and he sometimes performed exorcisms using them.[4]

---

[4] Adapted from various accounts in Abbe François Trochu, *The Curé de Ars: St. Jean-Baptiste Marie Vianney* (Charlotte, N.C.: TAN Books, 2007), 250–73.

On one occasion, a demon-possessed woman, ranting and screaming, was brought to him by her husband, who lived at some distance. After the curé studied the situation, he insisted that she be taken to the bishop. At that point, the woman was able to speak, and she said in a chilling voice, "If I had the power of Jesus Christ, I would plunge you all into hell."

The priest commanded her to be silent and told some of the men who were watching to take her to the foot of the high altar in the church nearby. Her violence and unnatural strength required four men to restrain her.

Once she was in the church, the saint placed his reliquary on her head. She immediately became as rigid as a corpse. A few minutes later she stood up unassisted, walked around, blessed herself with holy water, and knelt to pray. She was completely cured.

The Dancing Demoniac

Another demon-possessed woman once sang and danced all day in front of the church at Ars as a form of mockery. When the man who served as John's bodyguard made her drink a few drops of holy water, she immediately began to scream in fury and bite the walls of the church. Her son had come with her, and he could only stand by helplessly as a priest led her to the place between the rectory and the church where John would have to pass.

When the curé saw her and drew close, he gave her a blessing. Instantly she became calm. Later her son declared that she had been possessed for forty years, and never before had she seemed so furious, and afterward so peaceful.

A Teacher Is Delivered

On yet another occasion, a young schoolteacher in the city of Orange was exhibiting symptoms of demon possession. The archbishop of Avignon studied the case and recommended that she be taken to John. So she was brought to the saint by the vicar of Saint-Pierre of Avignon and the superior of the Franciscan nuns in Orange.

When they arrived in Ars, she was taken to the sacristy, where the curé was preparing for Mass. She immediately became disturbed and tried to leave, insisting that the sacristy was too crowded. John indicated to the others to leave the two of them there alone, so they left the room.

The vicar stood just outside the door, however, so he could hear what was said on the other side. The saint asked, "You absolutely insist that you must leave?"

"Yes," the demon replied.

"Why?"

"Because I'm with a man I don't like."

"So you don't like me?" John asked.

"No!" the demon shrieked.

Apparently the curé blessed her, because right away, she opened the door and came out weeping joyfully.

"I'm afraid it will come back," she said to John. But he assured her that she was safe. The demon never returned, and she was able to go back to teaching in Orange.

* * * *

God's Foolishness Triumphs

In all these ways, the Curé of Ars shone the light of God into the dark shadows that had been left behind by the Enlightenment. A simple peasant who could hardly complete his studies became a spiritual warrior more powerful against the Evil One than all the celebrated intellects of that movement.

His life illustrated powerfully the Apostle's declaration: "God chose what is foolish in the world to shame the wise, God chose what is weak in the world to shame the strong" (1 Cor 1:27–28).

- CHAPTER 17 -

ST. GEMMA GALGANI
Victim Soul, Valiant Soldier
(1878–1903)

Take your share of suffering as a good soldier of Christ Jesus.
2 Timothy 2:3

Napoleon's thirst for empire and glory compelled him to spend most of his time at war. Once again, Europe bled, and the continent was bathed in misery. Yet even the awful disasters of the belligerent Corsican's wars, and dozens of others in the nineteenth century, could not compare in horror to the conflicts that awaited in the twentieth. Satan had much to celebrate.

Sometime in the years between the Russo-Turkish War and World War I, Our Lord spoke to a young Italian woman from Tuscany named Gemma Galgani. He said:

> My child, I have need of victims, and strong victims! In order to appease the just wrath of My divine Father, I need souls who, by their sufferings, tribulations, and difficulties, make amends for sinners and for their ingratitude. Oh, that I could make all understand how incensed My heavenly Father is by the impious world! There is nothing to stay His hand, and He is now preparing a great chastisement for all the world.

Gemma responded with heroic generosity. "I am the victim," she said, "and Jesus the sacrificing priest. Act quickly, O Jesus! All that Jesus wills, I desire. Everything that Jesus sends me is a gift." [1]

A Victim Soul

These words may be puzzling to those who are accustomed to think only of God's mercy. The warning of Our Lord to Gemma may seem too harsh and His call for victims unsettling. If so, however, we need only ponder a few of the vast criminal horrors of our time, diabolically inspired: the Holocaust of the Jews; Stalin's forced mass starvation of his own people; unborn babies ripped apart in their mother's wombs by the millions; the outrage of children beheaded, raped, and crucified by Islamic terrorists.

Do these atrocities stir in us a righteous anger? If not, our souls are dead. If so, how much more wrath would they provoke in the heart of a perfectly holy God?

Yet even if we accept that our Father in heaven is incensed by heinous crimes on earth, we may still question the words that Gemma heard. Would God's Son, who Himself suffered terribly for the sins of the world, call for willing victims to make reparations for that sinful world as well? Can our sufferings actually become redemptive in that way?

According to age-old Catholic tradition, the answer is yes.

What Christian would claim that Christ's suffering was insufficient to save the world? Nevertheless, beginning with St. Paul, many Christians have affirmed that He has chosen to allow the members of His body to be joined to Him so intimately that His suffering becomes ours and ours becomes His, for the benefit of others.

The Apostle put it this way: "Now I rejoice in my sufferings for your sake, and in my flesh I complete what is lacking

---

[1] Venerable Father Germanus, C.P., *The Life of St. Gemma Galgani*, trans. A. M. O'Sullivan (St. Louis: B. Herder, 1913), 175–76.

in Christ's afflictions for the sake of His body, that is, the Church" (Col 1:24).

We have been promised in Scripture that salvation means we become "partakers" in God's own nature (see 2 Pt 1:4). Should we be surprised if that participation may include a share in His redemptive work through suffering?

The French scholar Abbé Paulin Giloteaux, writing about victim souls only a few years after Gemma's death, summarized the sacred calling this way:

> In the darkest hours of this world's history, when godlessness is rife or immorality parades itself before men's eyes, it pleases God to summon certain souls to sacrifice themselves, freely, in imitation of the Crucified, for the advantage of the Church and the salvation of the world. He visits them with sorrows and afflictions, trials and sufferings, physical, moral and supernatural, inviting them in secret, by His grace, to reproduce within themselves the state of the Redeemer's soul throughout His passion, so causing them to be, like Jesus, mediators, expiating and atoning.[2]

Suffering Was Her Weapon

We gaze here, of course, into a profound mystery, never fully grasped in this world. But gaze we must if we hope to understand and appreciate even a little of Gemma's extraordinary suffering. In the lives of many other holy men and women, the triumphs in spiritual combat seem clear to us, if sometimes delayed. But the victim soul, as tradition calls those like Gemma Galgani, seems more like a soldier on a noble suicide mission.

---

[2] Abbé Paulin Giloteaux, *Victim Souls: A Doctrinal Essay*, trans. L. M. G. Bond (London: Bournes, Oates & Washbourne, 1927), ix–x.

The victim has no expectation of immediate victory. But the victim's total sacrifice, willingly offered, in the end helps turn the tide of the war.

We must keep all this in mind, then, as we consider the unrelenting diabolical assaults Gemma endured, with little or no relief in this life. To these were added, in fact, terrible afflictions of serious physical illness, the stigmata, and the scorn and rejection of many friends and family members. In the fierce spiritual combat to which she was called, her suffering was her mission, her strategy, her armor, her weapon.

No doubt, in the terrible world wars and persecutions of the Church in the twentieth century, the chastisement threatened by Our Lord still came. But we might shudder to imagine how much worse the horrors might have been if not for Gemma and other victim souls like her.

The Devil Opposes Her Prayers

Much of what we know about Gemma comes from her diary and from a biography written by her spiritual director. These works reveal the hidden life of a young Christian passionately devoted to Jesus and heroic in her acceptance of suffering for His sake and the sake of the world.[3]

*   *   *   *

According to her spiritual director, Our Lord once said to Gemma, "Be prepared, My child. At My bidding, by the war he will wage against you the Devil will be the one to put the last touch on the work that I will accomplish in you."

This war was total in that it was waged against all the virtues and holy activities by which this child of grace studied

---

[3] The following narrative, spanning several sections, is adapted from various accounts in St. Gemma's diary; Germanus (cited previously); and Fr. Amadeo, C.P., *Blessed Gemma Galgani*, trans. Fr. Osmund Thorpe, C.P. (London: Burns, Oates & Washbourne, 1935).

to advance in perfection. They were all hateful to Satan, and he attacked them all with unmitigated rage. It appeared to be almost his only aim to torment this servant of God by continually inventing new methods of assailing her.

Gemma learned that the best way to defend herself against the demons and to accomplish God's purposes is through prayer, which she practiced with all the fervor of her soul. And she derived the most remarkable benefits from it. But the Enemy stopped at nothing to prevent her from this holy discipline.

To wear her out, he would provoke her to weariness and loss of desire to pray. Then, when he found it impossible to make her lose sight of God, he caused her violent headaches that sent her to bed and kept her from prayer. In many other ways as well, he tried to distract her from praying.

"Oh!" she said, "what torment this gives me, not to be able to pray! What exhaustion it costs me! How many efforts does that wretch make to render it impossible for me to pray! Yesterday evening he tried to kill me, and he would have succeeded if Jesus hadn't come quickly to my aid. I was terrified and kept the image of Jesus in my mind, but I couldn't pronounce His name."

The Devil Blasphemes

At other times, the Devil varied the attack. "What are you doing?" he once said, blaspheming. "How stupid you are to pray to that evildoer! Look at the harm He does to you, keeping you nailed to the Cross with Himself! How can you care for Him, for someone you don't even know, who makes all who love Him suffer?"

But these and all his other evil suggestions were like dust before the wind. She was outraged by such blasphemies directed toward her Jesus.

In the midst of so much suffering, the servant of God found comfort in telling her spiritual director so that he could provide her direction and advice. This the wicked enemy could not bear, and he tried to turn her away from her spiritual guide. He depicted her director as an ignorant, fanatical, deluded man, and with many arguments, he strove to terrify her, hoping to convince the poor child that she herself was all but lost.

"For some days," Gemma once wrote, "*Chiappino* [her nickname for the Devil, which means 'burglar'] has pursued me in every guise and way and has done all in his power against me. This monster keeps on redoubling all his efforts to ruin me and tries to deprive me of anyone who directs or advises me. But even should this happen, I am not afraid."

War Against Her Spiritual Director

Seeing that all his efforts didn't succeed in shaking her confidence in her director, the Devil resorted to acts of violence. He assaulted her while she tried to persevere in writing her diary. He snatched the pen from her hand, tore up the paper, then dragged her from the table, seizing her by the hair with such violence that it came off in his brutal claws.

Then, withdrawing in fury, he shouted, "War, war against your spiritual father! War as long as he lives!"

"Believe me, Father," she said to her spiritual director, "to hear this despicable wretch, you would think that his fury was against you more than against me."

A Demon in the Confessional

Once the Devil pretended to be a priest to whom Gemma used to make her confession. She had gone one day to church, and while preparing herself to make her confession, she saw that the priest was already in the confessional. That puzzled her, because she hadn't seen him pass and enter there. At the same time, she felt extremely disturbed in spirit, as usually was the case when she was in the presence of the Evil One.

Nevertheless, she entered the confessional and began her confession as usual. The voice and ways were indeed those of the usual confessor, but his talk was foul and scandalous, accompanied by improper gestures.

"What has happened?" she exclaimed. She trembled, and when she regained her presence of mind, she left the confessional in a hurry. As she did, she saw that the pretended "confessor" had disappeared. It was in fact the Devil, who by his coarse and fiendish ways had sought to deceive her or at least make her lose all confidence in the minister of God.

Disguised as an Angel of Light

Failing in this attempt, the Enemy made another. He appeared to Gemma in the form of an angel, radiant with light, insinuating himself with the most subtle cunning in order to throw her off guard. As he had done with Eve in the Garden of Eden, he portrayed things in the most false of colors.

"Look here," he said. "I can make you happy if only you will swear to obey me." Gemma, who this time didn't feel in her soul the usual disturbance indicating the presence of the Devil, stood listening in her simplicity. But God came to her aid.

After the first wicked proposal, her eyes were opened. She stood up, exclaiming, "My God! Mary Immaculate! Make me die rather than that!" And with these words, she rushed toward the counterfeit "angel" and spat in his face. At that moment, she saw him vanish in the form of fire.

Temptations to Disobedience

One day Gemma wrote to her spiritual director about "a fresh assault" by the Enemy. The director had recently instructed her not to engage in certain severe penances.

"Listen, Father," she wrote. "Yesterday after confession, on my return to the house and as soon as I had a moment to myself, I knelt down, for it was the time of my prayer. Then I began to recite the Rosary of the Five Wounds of Jesus.

"At the fourth wound, I saw before me a figure like Jesus, freshly scourged all over, with his heart laid open and bleeding. He said to me:

'Is this the way, my child, that you repay me? Look at me; see how much I have suffered for you. And now instead you cannot give me the consolation of those penances you were told not to practice. They really aren't much; you can very well continue them as you did before.'

'No, no,' I replied, 'I wish to obey my spiritual director; and if I do what you desire, I will be disobeying.'"

Then she heard him say that she wasn't in the least obliged to obey her director and that she should do as he himself told her. She was just about to return to her penances when the *real* Lord intervened.

"Jesus helped me," she wrote. "I rose, took holy water, and became calm—not, however, without receiving a blow or two, which has been a frequent gift to me from Satan. And you know, Father, it was without doubt Satan who had appeared to me."

Discerning the Apparitions

Hoping to protect her from these satanic apparitions, her spiritual director told her—no matter which form that persons of the other world might appear to her—to begin at once to repeat the words, "Long live Jesus!" He was unaware that Our Lord Himself had given her a similar remedy in the words, "Blessed be Jesus and Mary!"

As an obedient child, in order to obey both instructions, she used to repeat both exclamations. The good angels always repeated her words, "Long live Jesus! Blessed be Jesus and Mary!" But the evil ones either refused to reply or pronounced only a few words, such as "Long live" or "Blessed," without adding either of the sacred names. In this way, Gemma was able to recognize them, and she scorned them accordingly.

Further Temptations

In order to prompt her to vanity, Satan sometimes caused Gemma to envision a crowd of spirits clad in white who placed themselves around her bed to offer her homage. At other times, he showed her that letters to her spiritual directors were being preserved by the religious authorities for some important purpose. Other apparitions carried with them a similar purpose.

But all were in vain. Gemma was not so easily seduced by vainglory, being solidly grounded in humility.

This spirit of darkness also made an attempt to shake her immense confidence in God. He strove accordingly during her periods of desolation and abandonment to renew in her mind the fear that she would be lost. "And don't you see," he said to her, "that Jesus doesn't hear you, and doesn't want to know anything more about you? Why weary yourself running after Him? Give it up, and resign yourself to your unhappy fate."

This was the most terrible temptation that agonized many of the greatest saints of the Church; Gemma also felt all its force. Yet she overcame it, either through the constant habit she had acquired of turning to God with lively faith in every spiritual trial or because of the special assistance given to her by God Himself.

In this way, she was able to say on one occasion, "The Devil, contemptible wretch that he is, tries his best. . . . But Jesus by His words gives me such tranquility that, with all his efforts, Satan hasn't been able to shake my confidence, not even for one moment."

Violent Assaults

The Devil, finding all his strategies made useless by this child, became furious. Throwing off the mask, he took to waging open war against her. He appeared to her repeatedly in horrible forms: at one time as a savage dog, at another as a hideous monster, again as a man in a rage.

He used to begin by terrifying her with his hideous and threatening appearance. Then he rushed on her, beat her, tore her with his teeth, threw her down, dragged her by the hair, and in other countless ways tortured her innocent body.

No one can attribute these things to mere hallucinations, for their effects were only too real: her hair scattered about the room, the bruises and livid marks that remained for days, the excessive pains she felt in all her limbs, and more. The noises that were heard, the blows endured, and the shaking of her bed, lifted up and then thrown down, were all too real.

Nor did these assaults and annoyances last only a few moments. They lasted for hours together without stopping and even throughout the whole night. Gemma provided in her diary some details about these occurrences:

"Today I thought I was to be entirely free from that nauseating beast, and instead he has knocked me around brutally. I had gone to bed with the firm intention of sleeping, but it turned out otherwise. He began with powerful blows that made me fear I should die.

"He was in the form of a great black dog. He put his paws on my shoulders, making every bone in my body ache. At times I believed that he would maul me. Then one time, when I was taking holy water, he twisted my arm so cruelly that I fell to the earth in great pain. The bone was dislocated, but Jesus touched me and it went back into place.

"After a while, I remembered that I had around my neck the relic of the Holy Cross. Making the Sign of the Cross, I became calm. Jesus let me see Himself, but only for a short time, and He strengthened me anew to suffer and struggle."

Beaten With a Stick

In a letter, Gemma wrote: "Yesterday, too, the Devil knocked me around. Aunt told me to draw a bucket of water to fill the room jugs. I was walking with the jugs in my hands, passing by the image of the Heart of Jesus, and offering Him fervent acts of love.

"Suddenly I received such a strong blow of a stick on my left shoulder that I fell. Nothing was broken. But even today I feel very unwell, and everything I do seems to give me pain."

In yet another letter, again she wrote: "Once more I have passed a bad night. The Devil appeared before me as a giant of great height. He beat me fiercely all night, and kept saying to me: 'For you there is no more hope of salvation; you are in my hands.'

"I replied that God is merciful, and so I feared nothing. Then, giving me a hard blow on the head, he said in a rage, 'May you be accursed!' and disappeared.

"I went to my room to rest a little, and there I found him. He began again to strike me with a knotted rope, and he kept on because he wanted me to listen to him while he suggested wickedness. I said no, and he struck harder, knocking my head violently against the ground.

"At a certain moment it came to my mind to invoke Jesus' Holy Papa. [This is how she used to speak of the Eternal Father.] I called aloud: 'Eternal Father, through the most precious Blood, free me!'

"I don't quite know what happened next. That disgusting beast dragged me violently from my bed and threw me, dashing my head against the floor with such force that it hurts me still. I became senseless and remained lying there until I came to myself a long time afterward. Jesus be thanked!"

The Holy Name Triumphs

It would take too long to recount all these painful scenes. They happened very often and sometimes continued for days. The poor victim had become in a certain sense accustomed to them and, beyond the bodily sufferings they caused her, she ceased to be alarmed at them.

She regarded the hellish monster with a serenity like that of a dove. Until her spiritual director forbade it, she sometimes used to answer the monster contemptuously. But when he was finally overcome by the invocation of the Holy Name of Jesus, he was forced to leave. He shuffled away in a hurry, and the simple child followed him with jubilant laughter.

"If you could only have seen him, Father," she wrote, "how he ran, and how often he tripped as he fled, and gave vent to his rage, you too would have laughed at him. How terribly he smells, like burnt sulfur, and how horrible to look at! But Jesus has told me not to fear him."

The Devil Appears as a Cat

Once her spiritual director was assisting her when she was ill and in danger of death. After he had sat down in a corner of the room to pray the office, before long, he heard and saw passing by him a large, dark, furious-looking cat. After dashing round the room, it jumped up on the foot of the iron bed, directly in front of the sick girl, and crouched there with a savage stare.

Her director later recalled, "I felt my blood curdle at the sight, but Gemma remained quite calm. Trying to hide my fear, I said to her: 'What's the matter now?'

"'Don't be afraid, Father,' she replied. 'It's that vile demon who wants to annoy me. But don't worry, because he won't do you any harm.'"

He approached her, trembling, with holy water and sprinkled her bed. The demon vanished, leaving her in perfect serenity as if nothing had happened.

Fears of Displeasing Jesus

What really frightened her was the fear of offending God by yielding to Satan's malicious suggestions. Although she was aware of having always thus far resisted, the danger nonetheless seemed to her to be always imminent, and it kept her almost beside herself with fear. There was no remedy that she overlooked to defend herself against those satanic assaults—crosses, relics of saints, scapulars, special prayers, and above all, a daughter's loving recourse to God, to His heavenly Mother, to her angel guardian, and to her spiritual director.

"Come quickly, Father," she once wrote to her spiritual director, "or at least repeat the minor exorcisms at a distance. The Devil is doing all he can against me. Help me save my soul, because I'm afraid that I'm already in the power of Satan.

"Oh, if you only knew how much I'm suffering! Last night how self-satisfied he was! He took me by the hair and tore it away, saying, 'Disobedience, disobedience! Now there is no more time to repent. Come, come with me!'

"He wanted to take me to hell. He stayed there more than four hours tormenting me, and that's how I passed the night. I fear so much that listening to him I may displease Jesus."

A Diabolical Invasion

It happened at times, though very rarely indeed, that the evil spirit was allowed to invade her whole person. It bound up the powers of her soul and disturbed her imagination to such a degree that she seemed almost obsessed.

On such occasions, she was most pitiful to see. She herself had developed such a horror of this deplorable condition that the bare thought of it made her grow pale and tremble.

"Oh, God!" she said. "I have been in hell, without Jesus, without Mary, without my angel. If I've come out of it without sin, I owe it, Jesus, to You alone. And yet I'm contented, because in suffering in this way, and suffering ceaselessly, I know that I'm doing Your most holy will."

No doubt, if attacks of this kind had been often repeated or had lasted for a considerable time, the poor sufferer—even though perfectly resigned to her affliction—would have died from the anguish.

Temptations to Impurity

In her diary, Gemma once wrote: "It happened today as usual. I had gone to bed; in fact, I was asleep. But the Devil didn't like that.

"He presented himself in a disgusting manner. He tempted me, but I was strong. I commended myself to Jesus, asking that He take my life rather than allow me to offend Him.

"What horrible temptations those were! All temptations displease me, but those against holy purity make me most wretched. Afterward, he left me in peace, and the angel guardian came and assured me that I had not done anything wrong.

"I complained somewhat, because I wanted his help at such times. He said that whether I saw him or not, he would be always above my head."

"Don't Pray for Sinners!"

Satan often appeared to Gemma with eyes of fire, saying in threatening tones, "While acting for yourself, do as you please. But listen well: Do nothing for the conversion of sinners. If you attempt it, I'll make you pay dearly for it."

At other times, feigning the role of prudent counselor, he would say, "What makes you so presumptuous? You're laden with sins, and all the years of your life wouldn't be enough to mourn and atone for them. Yet you lose time praying about the sins of others?

"Don't you see that your own soul is in danger? A strange gain this is, thinking of others and neglecting yourself."

Once she was heard to say to Our Lord in ecstasy, "Do You wish to know, Jesus, who has forbidden me to think about sinners? The Devil. On the contrary, Jesus, I recommend them to You. Think of them, O Jesus, all poor sinners, and teach me to do as much as possible to save them."

On another occasion, the hellish demon said, "Don't you see that Jesus no longer hears you and that He will no longer have anything to do with you?" But through the grace of God, and with Gemma exercising her will, all the Devil's attempts to tempt Gemma were made in vain.

*   *   *   *

Gemma's Death

The Enemy of her soul made one last attempt to make her stumble as she lay dying of tuberculosis at the age of twenty-five. Evil spirits tormented her imagination with fantasies calculated to provoke fear, sadness, anxiety, and revulsion. The many trials of her life were paraded through her memory as the demons tried to lead her to despair.

Next came bodily injuries and phantoms of horrible beasts attacking her: loathsome insects crawling over her food, serpents slithering around her body and trying to crush her. With no priest present to rebuke the demons, she did it herself. Then she cried out to heaven for help.

From time to time, Our Lord or her guardian angel came to comfort her. Once, Jesus told her, "Why, My child, instead of being intimidated by those attacks, don't you increase your hope in Me? Always resist and never yield. If the temptation lasts, maintain your resistance. In this way the battle will lead you to victory." [4]

---

[4] Germanus, 312–17.

Gemma did indeed increase her hope in God, and she continued to defy her enemies by exclaiming, "Long live Jesus! All for Jesus only!" On Good Friday in 1903, she at last went on to her reward, echoing the words of Jesus from the Cross: "I commend my poor soul to You, Jesus!" Her mission was accomplished—or so it seemed.

A New Field of Combat

Soon after Gemma's death, the miracles began. It became clear that on her new field of combat as part of the Church Triumphant, she was to assist her comrades still battling as soldiers in the Church Militant. As the knowledge began to spread of her hidden life of holiness, and especially of her warfare with the powers of darkness, those who sought relief from diabolical activity often called on her assistance, with remarkable results.

More than a century later, she still comes to the aid of those possessed by demons. In 2005, an exorcist reports, in the middle of the Rite of Exorcism, the female victim cried out in a deep, guttural voice, "No! The one in black is here—the jinx!"

The exorcist knew from past exorcisms with other victims that this was the demons' jargon for Gemma Galgani. She had come once again to the assistance of someone being cruelly tormented, because she knew firsthand the woman's sufferings. With her help, the victim was delivered.[5]

---

[5] Matt Baglio, *The Rite: The Making of a Modern Exorcist* (New York: Doubleday, 2009), 2.

- CHAPTER 18 -

ST. PIO OF PIETRELCINA
Adorned With the Victor's Crown
(1887–1968)

Behold, Satan demanded to have you, that he might sift you like wheat; but I have prayed for you, that your faith may not fail; and when you have turned again, strengthen your brethren.
Luke 22:31-32

In warning St. Gemma of "a great chastisement for all the world," Our Lord had called for multiple victim souls whose sufferings, willingly endured, could lighten the sufferings of others. She died, having accomplished her mission, before the horrors of the twentieth century began. But one of her younger contemporaries, whose life spanned both world wars, answered the call as well.

He was born Francesco Forgione, but the world would come to know him as Padre Pio.[1] Francesco was the son of devout peasant farmers in the village of Pietrelcina in southern Italy. His family attended Mass daily, prayed the Rosary each evening, and fasted three days a week. From a young age, he began preparing himself for an extraordinary life.

---

[1] The following account is drawn from C. Bernard Ruffin, *Padre Pio: The True Story*, rev. ed. (Huntington, Ind.: Our Sunday Visitor, 1991); Renzo Allegri, *Padre Pio: Man of Hope* (Ann Arbor, Mich.: Servant, 2000); and Charles Mortimer Carty, *Padre Pio: The Stigmatist* (repr., Charlotte, N.C.: TAN Books, 2010).

By the time he was five, Francesco had already decided to consecrate his life to God. He took on penances that most adults would find daunting. Among other disciplines, he slept on a stone floor with a stone for his pillow.

Francesco's mother reported that as a child he could see and have conversations with Jesus, Mary, and his guardian angel. It seemed to him such a normal state of affairs that he assumed others could do the same. But he saw other, less comforting, visitors as well. Even when he was still young enough to sleep in a crib, he later recalled, after his mother turned off the lights and left him alone, he saw demons who made him scream in terror.[2]

At the age of ten, Francesco decided to become one of the Capuchins, a Franciscan order. But he had to receive some years of education before the order would receive him. After several years, he was able to complete the necessary study.

A Vision of the Battle

On New Year's Day in 1903, when he was fifteen, Francesco was pondering his vocation, wondering whether he could make the necessary sacrifices to live such a life. Suddenly his physical senses were suspended, and he received a vision within his mind. What he saw recalls the vision of St. Perpetua in the arena many centuries before.

In the vision, Francesco "beheld a majestic man of rare beauty, resplendent as the sun." The man took him by the hand and said, "Come with me, for you must fight a doughty warrior." Then he led him to a vast field where he saw a great multitude divided into two groups.

On one side was a host of handsome men dressed in white. On the other were men whose faces were hideous and who were dressed in black. Between them was a large

---

[2] Fernando da Riese, *Padre Pio da Pietrelcina crocifisso senza croce* (San Giovanni Rotondo: Edizioni Padre Pio, 2008), 51.

space where a giant appeared, dark and terrifying, "so tall that his forehead seemed to touch the heavens."

As the giant approached, the guide informed Francesco that this was the creature he would have to engage in combat. Francesco was terrified and nearly fainted. His guide helped support him with his arm, but Francesco begged to be spared such a contest, because the giant's strength was much too great to be overcome.

Nevertheless, the guide insisted that Francesco must fight the warrior. If he entered the contest in faith, the guide would remain with him, and he would win. The reward for his victory would be a shining crown for his brow.[3]

Francesco Is Victorious

Francesco engaged the giant in combat. Though the struggle was fierce and his opponent ferocious, with the help of his guide, Francesco was victorious. Then his guide placed on the victor's head a crown of indescribable beauty.

Suddenly, the guide withdrew the crown. He told Francesco that he would have an even more beautiful crown waiting for him if he would continue the fight against the giant. Though he had won this battle, the adversary would try again and again to overcome him.

"Fight valiantly and do not doubt my aid," said the guide. "Keep your eyes wide open, for that mysterious personage will try to take you by surprise. Do not fear his . . . formidable might, but remember what I have promised you: that I will always be close at hand and I will always help you, so that you will always succeed in conquering him."

With the giant defeated, the host of hideous-looking men fled, cursing and screaming. But the multitude of

---

[3] Pio of Pietrelcina, *Epistolario I: Corrispondenza con le diretorri spirituali (1910–1922)* (San Giovanni Rotondo, 1973), 1281–82, quoted in Ruffin, 40–41.

handsome men erupted into applause and praise for the beautiful youth who had assisted Francesco. Then the vision ended.[4]

The guide in the vision, of course, was Jesus Christ, and the adversary was the Devil. As it had been with St. Perpetua, the spiritual combat portrayed was fierce, but the victory was assured. Yet one difference was clear: Perpetua's struggle was to be a single great combat with Satan, won in a matter of hours through her glorious martyrdom. Francesco's combat, on the other hand, was to be a perpetual struggle, a victory won only after a lifetime of spiritual warfare. And the war had begun.

The Battle Begins

A few days later, Francesco was received by the Capuchins and given the name Pio. His spiritual battle began then in earnest.

From the beginning of his novitiate, Pio suffered from a number of ailments that sometimes became quite serious and lasted for a lifetime. His digestive tract was easily irritated, and he had attacks of vomiting so severe that on occasion he would go for weeks without being able to retain solid food. He endured spasms of violent coughing, pains in his chest and back, frequent high fevers, and pounding headaches.

The novice's superiors sought medical advice to discover the cause of his ailments. But they could never agree on a diagnosis, and the problems continued.

Pio worried that his illnesses might be God's punishment for his sins. But his spiritual director, Fr. Benedetto Nardella, reassured him, saying, "Your sufferings are not punishment, but rather ways of earning merit that the Lord is giving you, and the shadows that weigh on your soul are

---

[4] *Epistolario I*, 194, quoted in Ruffin, 40.

generated by the Devil, who wants to harm you. . . . The closer God draws to a soul, the more the Enemy troubles him."[5]

Meanwhile, Pio's mystical experiences continued. He experienced apparitions and locutions from heavenly visitors, and he demonstrated spiritual gifts such as bilocation, levitation, and knowledge of hidden matters. But he was also assaulted by demonic powers. His brother friars sometimes heard screams or roars coming from his room at night.

One summer night, the young man had trouble sleeping because of the heat and humidity. He heard footsteps in the next room, as if a man were pacing back and forth. *He can't fall asleep*, he thought. *I'll call him and we can at least chat for a while.*

Pio went to the window to call to his friend, but before he could open his mouth, he saw a huge black dog, with an immense head and furious eyes, standing on the sill of the window of the room where he had heard the noises. Before he could react, the hideous dog jumped onto the roof and disappeared. The next day, Pio learned that the room was unoccupied.[6]

"A Perfect Victim"

Despite his health problems, which had inescapably made his studies more difficult, Pio was ordained a priest in August of 1910, at the age of twenty-three. Holy cards were distributed to those who attended the ordination, with a prayer the young man had written: "With Thee, may I be for the world the way, the truth, and the life, and through Thee, a holy priest, a perfect victim."[7]

---

[5] *Epistolario I*, 194, quoted in Ruffin, 73.

[6] Allegri, 35.

[7] Ruffin, 74.

Four weeks after his ordination, Padre Pio received for the first time a form of the stigmata, the wounds of Christ appearing on his own body. After a short time, they became invisible, but he could still feel the pain. Our Lord was providing him a seal of his sacrifice as a victim soul, a seal that would later become visible again.

Meanwhile, Satan's assaults continued and intensified. The saint suffered especially from temptations to impurity, fears of unconfessed sins, and despair about his salvation. Nevertheless, Our Lord provided consolations as well. The priest once wrote to his spiritual director: "All the ugly fantasies that the Devil introduces to my mind vanish when I abandon myself to the arms of Jesus. . . . I suffer immensely, but it is a grief that does me good." [8]

The young priest wrote as well of an inexplicable spiritual joy that supported him in his trials. He found he could repel the malicious attacks of the Enemy's temptations more and more easily as he offered himself to God.

Soon that gift to Our Lord took on a new meaning, three months after his ordination. With his spiritual director's permission, he made an explicit offering up of his life as a victim for poor sinners and for souls in purgatory. He placed himself on the Cross with Christ as a sacrifice to the Father in union with the Son.

Diabolical Apparitions

A few months later, Padre Pio wrote in a letter, "The Devil continues to wage war and doesn't show signs of giving up." [9] A number of diabolical apparitions took place in the following months. The holy man wrote:

> The ogre [his nickname for the Devil] won't admit defeat.
> He has appeared in almost every form. For the past few

---

[8] Ruffin, 76.
[9] *Epistolario I*, 215.

days he has paid me visits along with some of his satellites armed with clubs and iron weapons and, what is worse, in their own form as devils. I cannot tell you how many times he has thrown me out of bed, and dragged me around the room. But never mind! Jesus, our dear Mother, my little angel, St. Joseph, and our Father Francis are almost always with me.[10]

Because of his ailments, Padre Pio was sent back to Pietrelcina for a time in hopes that his native air would be more conducive to his healing. While he was there, the demons would often harass him in his bedroom at night. Sometimes the noise of these battles was so loud that people could hear it over a great distance. On occasion, neighbors were so frightened that they would flee from their homes.

The next morning, Padre Pio's mother would find the room in total chaos. The bed, the mattress, and the chairs would be turned over. The priest himself would be covered with bruises.

Even after Padre Pio returned to join the friars again, the noises continued for months, with blows on the walls. Ceramic pots and wooden chairs were broken without anyone touching them. Finally the saint's oldest brother sent for an exorcist, and peace returned to the house.[11]

In the days to come, Satan attacked Padre Pio under many forms and with many disguises, testing him with various temptations and assailing him with obscene insults. The Enemy appeared to him as dancing, naked young girls; as a young friend of the monks; as a crucifix; as the spiritual father or provincial father of the monks; as Pope Pius X; as a guardian angel; as St. Francis of Assisi; and even as the Blessed Virgin.

---

[10] *Epistolario I*, Letter to Padre Agostino, January 18, 1912, quoted in Michael Freze, S.F.O., *They Bore the Wounds of Christ: The Mystery of the Sacred Stigmata* (Huntington, Ind.: Our Sunday Visitor, 1989), 138.

[11] Allegri, 43-43.

Once Satan appeared accompanied by a whole army of demonic spirits. Another night, the demons pulled off his nightshirt so that they could beat him naked and leave him shivering in the cold. On yet another occasion, the saint was covered with spittle from the Devil.[12]

The Devil Counterfeits the Saint's Confessor

When unclean spirits tried to deceive him, how did Padre Pio see through their disguises? Whenever the apparitions were not of God, he felt a deep sense of disgust. In addition, he would tell them to praise Jesus. If they refused, he knew they were demonic.

One such episode from his years at the friary of San Giovanni Rotondo illustrates this strategy. During this time, Padre Pio's close friend, the professor Fr. Agostino, was hearing his confession daily. But one morning, he told the saint that he had no time for it till evening, so he should go ahead to Mass. When Agostino returned to Padre Pio's cell that night, he was surprised to find that the young man seemed to be suspicious of him.

"Are you my professor?" the saint asked.

"Of course I am!" replied Agostino. "Why would you ask such a peculiar thing?"

Padre Pio looked at him and demanded, "Say, 'Praise Jesus!'"

"Praise Jesus a thousand times! Now tell me what has happened."

So Padre Pio told him how, just after Agostino had left his cell in the morning, he answered a knock at the door to find the professor standing there—or so he thought. But the saint felt a surprising sense of revulsion at the man, and even though he looked like the professor, there was a wound on his forehead that had not been there before.

---

[12] These anecdotes are gathered from various accounts in St. Pio's correspondence in the *Epistolario*. See also Ruffin, 101–2.

"What happened to your forehead?" he asked.

"I fell while I was going downstairs. Now, son, I am here to hear your confession."

Given his discomfort, Padre Pio told him, "Say, 'Praise Jesus!'"

But the demon, who had taken the form of the friar's best friend, refused and vanished before his eyes.[13]

Exorcisms

The holy man did not simply remain on the defensive with the ancient Enemy. He also performed exorcisms. More than once, before the demon left the body of the possessed person, it would cry out, "Padre Pio, you give us more trouble than St. Michael!"

At other times, the unclean spirit would say, "Padre Pio, don't steal the bodies from us, and we won't bother you!" But despite the ferocity of their assaults on him, their offer to leave him alone never enticed him to cease the exorcisms.[14]

Once a possessed woman was waiting for the saint and the altar boys in the sacristy of a church after Vespers and Benediction. When Padre Pio entered the room, she began screaming curses and obscenities, but he was unperturbed. He took up the liturgical book and began the Rite of Exorcism.

Suddenly the woman shrieked and levitated, rising in the air about three feet and remaining there. Others who were present fled in terror, but the priest continued the exorcism in great tranquility. At last conquered, the demon himself fled the church.[15]

In another case of possession, a young wife had lain in a coma for an entire year. One evening she was carried into

---

[13] Ruffin, 85–86.

[14] See various accounts in St. Pio's correspondence in the *Epistolario*.

[15] Ruffin, 204.

the church during Vespers. She suddenly awoke from the coma while Padre Pio was blessing the congregation with the Blessed Sacrament. Immediately she began snorting like a bull.

According to witnesses, her body then started to swell up like a balloon. After Vespers, the saint brought the woman and her husband into the sacristy and began the Rite of Exorcism. As he was praying, the woman continued to snort and swell, and she tried to claw him.

When Padre Pio had finished, she calmed down and returned to her normal size. She took her husband's hand and wondered why she looked so untidy. Then she asked for a comb to fix her hair and walked out.[16]

The Madonna Comes to His Aid

In 1964, just a few years before Padre Pio went to his reward, an eighteen-year-old girl was brought to him with symptoms of demonic possession. Another priest had tried to perform an exorcism, but she became so violent that it took four strong men to restrain her from injuring him. The priest had recommended that she go to Padre Pio.

Performing an exorcism can be physically exhausting. Because the saint was by then too old for such an undertaking, he blessed the girl and left it to two younger priests who had been appointed by the bishop. They began the rite, but the girl became so violent that they had to stop after only a few minutes.

Padre Pio heard that the exorcism had been unsuccessful, so he decided to pray for the girl all night. At ten o'clock, his superior heard a crash in the saint's room. He and another brother found him lying on the floor there in a pool of blood.

---

[16] Ruffin, 205.

The holy man's face was swollen and battered, with a deep cut on his forehead and blood pouring from his nose. Yet there were no signs that anyone had forced an entry to the room, and nothing inside was damaged or even disturbed. However, a pillow that was usually sitting in an armchair was beneath the injured priest's head on the floor.

The superior sent the other brother for a doctor and asked Padre Pio who had tucked the pillow under his head. The saint whispered, "The Madonna." [17]

"The Hooves of Lucifer"

The next morning, the possessed teenager was in the square outside the church, among the crowd waiting to attend the Mass to be celebrated by Padre Pio. She screamed, "Last night I really hit that old man! You'll see if he comes down to Mass."

Everyone ignored her raving. But when the announcement was made that Padre Pio would not be presiding, the girl shrieked, "Did you hear? The old man will not come down to say Mass. I beat him up last night!" It would have been impossible, of course, for the girl to have gained entrance to the saint's room.

One woman in the crowd reported that she had heard the girl scream, "Pio, I've known you since you were small!" According to one report, when the exorcisms were resumed by the younger priests, they asked the demon in the victim, "Where were you last night?"

"I was upstairs to see the old man I hate so much," she replied, "because he is a source of faith. I would have done more, only the White Lady stopped me."

Several days later, Padre Pio was able to celebrate Mass again. When he came into the church, the girl was there; she screamed and fainted. She regained consciousness a few

[17] Ruffin, 366.

minutes later, and when she did, she was peaceful. Apparently, she had been delivered.

Two years later, a woman whose confession the saint was hearing said to him, "The last time I was here was when that little devil hurt you so much."

"*Little* devil!" exclaimed Padre Pio. "He wasn't little at all! He had the hooves of Lucifer to beat me with!" [18]

The Last Battle

In the saint's final years, the demonic apparitions and assaults seem to have lessened. But toward the very end, as his health failed, they returned with intensity. "The devils won't leave me alone for one minute!" he told a brother friar. But he also received consolations from heaven and was seen to experience ecstasies as he prayed alone in his room.

The wounds of his stigmata were slowly disappearing. To some, those wounds had been spiritual battle scars, and their disappearance was a sign that his mission on earth was accomplished.

On September 23, 1968, Padre Pio breathed his last after suffering a heart attack. As a fellow friar administered Last Rites, he died with these words on his lips: "Jesus . . . Mary . . . Jesus . . . Mary." His final battle was won, and his Lord and his Lady were coming to take him home from the battlefield.

---

[18] Ruffin, 367.

- EPILOGUE -

A WORLD ON FIRE

In his last years, Padre Pio had often lamented all the indicators that the culture of the West was lapsing into a post-Christian condition. The far-reaching immorality and materialism that had become so evident in the 1960s grieved him deeply and brought him to the edge of despair for the world. He abhorred miniskirts and the moral corruption of mass media entertainment, once insisting that "the Devil is in the cinema." He observed with dismay that the family was under spiritual assault.

Conditions in the Church after the Second Vatican Council also brought him great sorrow. After widespread criticism, even by Catholics, of *Humanae Vitae*—the courageous 1968 papal encyclical that reaffirmed the Church's condemnation of artificial contraception—he wrote a letter to Blessed Pope Paul VI. The saint, only a few weeks from death, stated his firm support and offered his daily sufferings on the Pope's behalf.[1]

Padre Pio was especially troubled by the dissent and unbelief that was manifest throughout the Church. The decline in vocations, even among the Capuchins, distressed

---

[1] Ruffin, 373.

him. The open revolt of so many priests and the religious scandalized him.

The saint who had so often demonstrated prophetic gifts appeared to have seen in his last days a vision of the world's future that horrified him. Many reports circulating insisted that he prophesied global catastrophe in the years to come. What we do know for sure is that when he was asked about the days ahead, he would often answer, "Can't you see that the world is catching on fire?" [2]

We would do well to ponder that question. The ancient Enemy seems to have once again intensified his attacks on a world that has lost its way and is wandering into his embrace. What must be our response?

In a letter once written to Fr. Agostino, Padre Pio issued a solemn warning to those who still fight in the ranks of the Church militant. That message is perhaps needed today more urgently than ever before:

> We must have no illusions about the Enemy, who is exceedingly strong, if we do not intend to surrender. In the light infused by God, the soul understands the great danger to which it is exposed if it is not continually on its guard. [3]

St. Pio and all the saints who have battled Satan through the ages stand in agreement on this essential matter. And the exhortation of the Apostle Paul to young Timothy (1 Tm 6:12) rings down the centuries to our own day: "Fight the good fight of the faith; take hold of the eternal life to which you were called."

---

[2] Ruffin, 364.
[3] Freze, 139.

BRIEF SCENES OF
SAINTS IN BATTLE

Our Blessed Lady

During the seventeenth-century beatification process for St. Frances de Sales, one of the Annecy Monastery visitation nuns made a formal statement about an exorcism she had witnessed. A young man had been possessed by a demon for five years, and the exorcism was being performed in the presence of the relics of St. Francis by Bishop Charles Auguste de Sales of Geneva, who was the saint's nephew and successor in the episcopal see.

According to her report, during one of the sessions, the demon shouted furiously, "Why should I leave?"

One of the visitation nuns present, perhaps frightened, invoked the Blessed Virgin: "Holy Mother of God, pray for us!"

On hearing those words, the demon screamed even more loudly: "Mary! Mary! There's no Mary for me! Don't say that name; it makes me shudder! If there were a Mary for me, as there is for you, I wouldn't be what I am! But for me there is no Mary! If I had just one instant of the many

[instants] that you people waste . . . ! Just one lone instant
and a Mary, and I would not be a demon!" [1]

The Desert Fathers (Early Centuries)

When St. Serapion was a youth and living with St. Theonas
in his desert hermitage, he developed the habit of stealing a
roll of bread after each meal and then eating it later in secret.
He wanted to stop sinning that way, but he was too ashamed
to say anything to his spiritual mentor.

One day St. Theonas commented to some visitors,
"Nothing harms the monks so much, and gives such happiness to the demons, as when he hides his thoughts from
his spiritual fathers." Under conviction, the boy began to
weep, pulled out the hidden roll from his pocket, threw
himself on the floor, and confessed what he had done. He
asked the old man to pray for him so that he would not
commit the sin again.

St. Theonas said, "My son, you are freed from your
bondage, even though I have said nothing to you. The
demon that, by your silence, you let dwell in your heart
has been killed because you confessed your sin. You let
him rule you because you never told him no; you never
rebuked him. From now on, he will never make a home
in you, because you have thrown him out of doors into
the open air."

Before the elder could finish speaking, his words came
to pass visibly. Something like a flame shot out of young
Serapion's breast, and it filled the house with its stench, so
that those present thought it was burning sulfur. The old
man said, "My son, behold the sign by which the Lord has
proven that I spoke truly—and you are free."

---

[1] Adapted from the account in Federico Suárez, *La Pasión de Nuestro Señor
Jesucristo*, 7th ed. (Madrid: Ediciones Rialp, 1993), 217–18.

Once when he was on a journey through Egypt, St. Macarius the abbot climbed into an ancient pagan cemetery to sleep for the night. He placed one of the mummies under his head as a pillow. The demons hated him because his faith in God made him unafraid of the place.

They tried to frighten him by calling out, "Lady, come with us to bathe!" Then another demon answered from beneath Macarius, as if he were the dead woman, "I have a pilgrim on top of me. So I can't move!"

The old man was undaunted. Confidently, he thumped the mummy and said, "Go ahead and get up, if you can!"

When the demons heard that, they screamed, "You've beaten us!" Then they fled in confusion because of the abbot's refusal to fear them.

The Devil once appeared to a monk disguised as an angel of light to deceive him by tempting him to pride. He announced, "I am the angel Gabriel, and I have been sent to you!"

But the monk was not deceived. He replied simply, "Better check and see: You must have been sent to someone else. I'm not worthy that an angel should be sent to me."

And so the Devil vanished—vanquished by the monk's humility.

A monk was once slapped on the cheek by a demon-possessed girl, so he followed the Lord's commandment and turned the other cheek to her. The demon was forced out of her by that simple action, and it began crying out, "Violence! The commandment of Jesus Christ is driving me out!" In that moment, the girl was healed.

Those present then went to some other monks to tell them what had happened. Giving glory to God, they said, "The pride of demons must fall before humble obedience to the commandments of Jesus Christ."

A monk once came to Abbot Sisois on the mountain of St. Anthony. He asked him, "Do you think that Satan persecuted the Christians of old as he persecutes us?"

Sisois answered, "Even more. For now his doom has drawn nearer, and he is upset."

The demons wanted to seduce an elderly monk, so they said to him, "Would you like to see Christ?"

He replied, "A curse be upon you and the one of whom you speak. I believe the words of my Christ, who said: 'If anyone says to you, "Behold, here is the Christ!" or "There He is!" do not believe it'" (see Mt 24:23).

Then they vanished, conquered by his knowledge of the Gospel and his faith in Christ.

Some people brought a demon-possessed man to an old monk to exorcise him. The monk said to the demon, "Get out of God's creature!"

The demon replied, "I'll go, but first I will ask you a question: Tell me, who are the goats, and who are the sheep?" (see Mt 25:31–46).

The old man said, "The goats are people like me. Who the sheep are, God alone knows."

At those words, the demon cried out, "Look! I must go out of him because of your humility!"

An old monk once said, "If anyone humbles himself by saying to his brother, 'Forgive me,' he will burn up the demons who tempt him."

A monk once asked the abbot St. Isidore of Crete, "Why are demons so violently afraid of you?"

He replied, "Ever since I became a monk, I have been trying not to let anger rise up in me to reach my mouth." [2]

St. Margaret of Cortona (1247–97)

One day a demon appeared to St. Margaret, attempting to terrify her. But her guardian angel appeared at the same moment, saying, "Don't be afraid, daughter, and don't lose courage! This demon has even less power to harm you than someone would have after he has been trampled underfoot by his conqueror. I am with you—I, the guardian angel of your soul, who is an exalted dwelling place of God." [3]

St. Catherine of Siena (1347–80)

People often brought to St. Catherine loved ones who were possessed by demons, seeking her help to cure them. Once an eight-year-old girl who was tormented by evil spirits was brought to her. St. Catherine had the girl kneel down with her and pray. She spent the whole night in prayer, in continual battle with the Enemy. The demon was so obstinate that the saint had to fight him until four in the morning.

The saint kept commanding the demon in the name of Jesus to depart, but he refused with unprecedented stubbornness. Eventually, the evil spirit recognized that he would have to leave the girl, so in order to frighten St. Catherine, he said to her, "If I come out of here, I will enter into you!"

Immediately the saint replied, "If the Lord wills it so— and I know that without His permission you can do nothing. God forbid that I should prevent you or in any other way alienate myself from His will or set myself up against Him."

Her humility took the proud demon by surprise, and he lost nearly all his power over the little girl. At last, he was

---

[2] Adapted from various translations of *The Sayings of the Fathers*.

[3] *The Guardian Angels: Our Heavenly Companions* (repr., Charlotte, N.C.: TAN Books, 2001), 22.

forced to leave, so as he did, he attacked the child's throat, causing it to swell. But St. Catherine made the Sign of the Cross on the child's neck, and she was healed.[4]

St. Colette (1381–1447)

During her childhood, St. Colette sometimes saw the Devil, and after she became an adult, he visited her often. Sometimes he appeared "in loathsome human guise" and at other times as cats, reptiles, and various other animals. The most common diabolical form she saw was a roaring black lion.

The lion frequently appeared to torment her when she was about to go to confession. One day when she was in the confessional, telling the priest what Satan had been doing, she concluded that if he himself could see the lion, he would better understand her experiences.

Colette could always see and hear the lion clearly prowling around her, but others could not. So she prayed that, just for a moment, the beast would be made manifest to her confessor. The Lord answered her prayer—and the priest promptly fainted![5]

St. Rita of Cascia (1381–1457)

The Devil often tried to distract St. Rita from her prayers by howling and appearing to her, but she dismissed him by making the Sign of the Cross. Once a woman was brought to her who had been possessed by demons for years. Moved by the woman's torments, the saint prayed for her and made

---

[4] Adapted from Blessed Raymond of Capua, *The Life of St. Catherine of Siena: The Classic on Her Life and Accomplishments as Recorded by Her Spiritual Director* (repr., Charlotte, N.C.: TAN Books, 2011), 216–21.

[5] Joan Carroll Cruz, *Angels and Devils* (Charlotte, N.C.: TAN Books, 2010), 172–73.

the Sign of the Cross on her head. Immediately, the demon was cast out, groaning and screaming.[6]

St. Joseph of Cupertino (1603–63)

On more than one occasion, St. Joseph's humble obedience to his superiors gave him leverage against unclean spirits. When they instructed him to cast out demons, he would command the Enemy to leave by saying, "Out of obedience I have come; therefore you must depart." The proud, rebellious devils were so flabbergasted by his childlike humility and obedience that they fled right away.

At other times, after praying the Litany of the Blessed Virgin, the humble saint would address the unclean spirits gently, saying, "I've come, not to drive you from this body, but only to obey. So if you wish to leave, do so; but if not, do as you like. For me it is sufficient to have obeyed." Once confronted by such humility, the haughty devils would leave immediately.

One night St. Joseph was praying at the tomb of St. Francis of Assisi. Suddenly the door of the basilica surrounding the tomb flew open violently and a stranger entered. St. Joseph noticed that he walked in an abnormally noisy way.

As the stranger approached, the lamps in the basilica went out one by one. When they all had been extinguished, the intruder was standing right next to St. Joseph. The man knocked the saint to the floor and tried to choke him.

Right away St. Joseph called to St. Francis for assistance. Then he saw St. Francis leave his tomb and light the lamps again, one by one, with a little candle. When the lamps were all flaming once more, the demon disappeared.[7]

---

[6] Cruz, 223.
[7] Cruz, 174, 254.

St. Margaret Mary Alacoque (1647–90)

One day, after Jesus had come to visit St. Margaret, a demon showed up. He was a dark and menacing figure, with eyes flashing like two burning coals as he gnashed his teeth at her. According to her autobiography, he said, "Since you're accursed, I'll capture you. Once I have you in my power, I'll make you feel what I can do! I'll injure you at every turn."

But his threats were in vain. "I nevertheless feared nothing," she wrote, "so great was the interior strength that I experienced . . . since I had beside me a small crucifix to which my Sovereign Deliverer had given the power to drive away from me all this hellish fury."[8]

St. Paul of the Cross (1694–1775)

St. Paul used a blessed rosary to free soldiers from demonic attacks on two occasions. In one case, a demon began dragging a soldier around his quarters. The saint heard the ruckus, ran to investigate, and discerned immediately that it was an evil spirit. He placed the holy rosary around the soldier's neck and commanded the demon to leave. The terrified soldier confessed his sins that very night, grateful to God for his deliverance.

In another case, a soldier was actually in the confessional when an invisible demonic power seized him and dragged him backward. The soldier gripped the confessional so firmly that, even with the priest still in it, it was almost dragged along with the frightened penitent. St. Paul was summoned and interrupted the assault by placing a rosary around the soldier's neck and his own mantle over the man. The soldier then went with the saint to the sacristy to make his confession.

Demons sometimes appeared to St. Paul in the form of cats who walked across his bed while he was trying to sleep.

---

[8] Cruz, 175.

At other times, they took the form of huge dogs or evil-looking birds. Once he saw the Devil appear as an immense and savage giant.

One of St. Paul's companions entered his room one day to pray with him. The companion could see the demonic giant, and he said, filled with fright, "Father, do you see?"

St. Paul, accustomed to such apparitions, replied simply, "Be quiet; don't be afraid. He hasn't come for you."[9]

St. Alphonsus Liguori (1696–1787)

Whenever evil spirits came to harass St. Alphonsus, he made the Sign of the Cross and commanded them to adore this sign of Christ's redemption of the human race. Then he recited these words from Scripture: "At the name of Jesus, every knee should bow, of those in heaven, on earth, and under the earth" (see Phil 2:10). The saint insisted that the demons had no patience to endure those words, so they fled.[10]

St. Anthony Mary Claret (1807–70)

During his seminary days, the young St. Anthony was once lying ill in bed with a severe cold. A demon began to tempt him by bringing to his mind memories of the world he had left behind. He inserted obscene images into his imagination and impure desires into his heart.

Anthony was deeply troubled. He had guarded his heart from previous temptations to impurity, but this time, the struggle was more intense than ever before. So he tried to make use of all the weapons that the saints and the masters of the spiritual life had recommended for this kind of combat.

---

[9] Cruz, 176, 233–34.
[10] Cruz, 233.

The young man tried diverting his attention to various objects. He made the Sign of the Cross, humbly calling on the Lord for protection. He took refuge with the Blessed Mother and prayed to his guardian angel and the saints for whom he felt a special devotion.

Nevertheless, the temptation continued, growing more intense by the minute. What else could he do to preserve his purity?

All of a sudden, a bright light filled his room. He looked up and saw the Queen of Angels, lovely and graceful, holding in her left hand a garland of roses. She took one of them with her right hand and pressed it to the forehead of a child kneeling beside her.

Then she said in a sweet, clear voice, "Anthony, this crown is for you, if you conquer." His heart was overwhelmed with joy.

A short time later, he had a vision of many saints praying. They were his heavenly patrons who were coming to his assistance by their intercession. But he also saw a herd of dragons creeping across the room, standing up and roaring as if they would swallow him alive.

All this lasted only a moment, and then the apparition vanished.

Every disturbing thought, memory, and image now fled from his mind. A great peace filled him instead. With the help of Our Lord and the saints, and especially the assistance of Our Lady, he had vanquished the Enemy and resisted his temptations. He knew that the crown of roses promised by the Blessed Mother was now on his head.

For many years afterward, he escaped any similar temptations to impurity. As he later recalled, "If later on I was tempted, it was in so insignificant a degree that it did not even merit the name of temptation." [11]

---

[11] Juan Echevarria, *The Miracles of St. Anthony Mary Claret: Archbishop and Founder* (repr., Rockford, Ill.: TAN Books, 1992), 28–29.

Blessed Mary Fortunata Viti (1827–1922)

Blessed Mary, a Benedictine nun, repelled demons by speaking the holy names of Jesus, Mary, or the Blessed Trinity. She was once heard to say, "Accursed hellish serpent, depart from me forever, in the name of the Most Holy Trinity, and of the Immaculate Mother of God who crushed your rebellious head." [12]

St. André of Montreal (1845–1937)

St. André was often visited by the Devil in the form of a large black cat. The visits usually came when the Holy Cross lay brother was preparing a body for burial. After performing this act of mercy, he usually had to endure a sleepless night. The cat would prowl around his room, rattling objects and making strange sounds.

When one of his lay brothers inquired about the cat, he answered, "The Devil doesn't like for me to do these good works. He's trying to frighten me." [13]

---

[12] Cruz, 233.

[13] Alden Hatch, *The Miracle of the Mountain* (New York: Hawthorne, 1959), 70.

SAINTLY WISDOM
FOR THE BATTLE

Our Lady's Help in the Battle

God has fashioned and shaped only one enmity, and that an irreconcilable one, which will endure and even increase, until the end: It is that between the Virgin Mary and the Devil, between the children and servants of the Blessed Virgin and the children and accomplices of Satan, so that the most terrible of the enemies of Satan created by God is Mary, his Blessed Mother.

St. Louis de Montfort

Not only is the most Blessed Virgin the queen of heaven and of all saints. She is also queen of hell and of all evil spirits. For she overcame them valiantly by her virtues.

From the very beginning God foretold the victory and empire that our queen would one day gain over the serpent, when he announced to him that a woman would come into the world to conquer him: "I will put enmity between you and the woman. . . . She will crush your head" [Gn 3:15]. And who could this woman, his enemy, be but Mary, who by her fair humility and holy life always conquered him and beat down his strength?

As St. Bernard remarks, this proud spirit, in spite of himself, was beaten down and trampled underfoot by this most Blessed Virgin. Now, as a slave conquered in war, he is forced always to obey the commands of this queen: "Beaten down and trampled under the feet of Mary, the Devil endures a wretched slavery." And she bound him in such a way that this enemy cannot stir so as to do even the least injury to any of those who go to her for protection.

"My children," Mary seems to say, "when the enemy assails you, fly to me. Cast your eyes on me, and be of good heart. Since I am your defender, victory is assured to you."

In this way, turning to Mary is a most secure means to conquer all the assaults of hell. For she is even the queen of hell and sovereign mistress of the demons, since she is the one who tames and crushes them. St. Bernardine of Siena expresses the thought this way: "The most Blessed Virgin rules over the regions of hell. She is therefore called the ruling mistress of the demons, because she brings them into subjection."

St. Alphonsus Liguori

Men do not fear a powerful, hostile army as much as the powers of hell fear the name and protection of Mary.

St. Bonaventure

Virgin Mother of God, you assist the dying, protecting them against the snares of the Devil; and you help them also after death, receiving their souls and conducting them to the kingdom of the blessed.

Blessed Raymond Jordano

Mary, most powerful Virgin, you are the mighty and glorious protector of the Church. In the midst of our anguish, our struggle, and our distress, defend us from the power of

the Enemy, and at the hour of our death receive our soul
into heaven.

St. John Bosco

The Devil is not satisfied with a soul turning against Jesus
Christ, unless it also turns from His Mother. Otherwise, the
Devil fears that the Mother will again, by her intercession,
bring back her Son.

St. Louis de Montfort

You, O Lady, by the simple invocation of your most powerful
name, give security to your servants against all the assaults
of the Enemy.

St. Germanus

The Blessed Virgin herself revealed to St. Bridget: "On earth
there is no sinner, however devoid he may be of the love of
God, from whom the Devil is not obliged to flee immediately, if he invokes her holy name with a determination to
repent." On another occasion she repeated the same thing
to the saint, saying, "All the demons venerate and fear her
name to such a degree, that on hearing it they immediately
loosen the claws with which they hold the soul captive."

Our Blessed Lady also told her: "In the same way as the
rebel angels fly from sinners who invoke the name of Mary,
so also do the good angels approach nearer to righteous
souls who pronounce her name with devotion." St. Germanus declares: "Just as breathing is a sign of life, so also is the
frequent pronunciation of the name of Mary a sign either
of the life of divine grace, or that it will soon come. For this
powerful name has in it the virtue of obtaining help and life
for him who invokes it devoutly."

To sum up, "This admirable name of our sovereign
Lady," says Richard of Saint Lawrence, "is like a fortified
tower. If a sinner takes refuge in it, he will be delivered from
death; for it defends and saves even the most abandoned."

But it is a tower of strength that not only delivers sinners from chastisement, but also defends the righteous from the assaults of hell.

St. Alphonsus Liguori

The demons tremble even if they only hear the name of Mary. St. Bernard declares that "in the name of Mary every knee bows," and "the devils not only fear but tremble at the very sound of that name."

As men fall prostrate with fear if a thunderbolt falls near them, so do the demons if they hear the name of Mary. Thomas à Kempis expresses the same sentiment in this way: "The evil spirits greatly fear the Queen of Heaven, and flee at the sound of her name, as if from fire. At the very sound of the word Mary, they are cast down as if by thunder."

O how many victories have those who turn to Mary gained only by making use of her most holy name! It was in this way that St. Anthony of Padua was always victorious. In this way also so many other lovers of this great queen conquered.

We learn from the history of the missions in Japan that many demons appeared under the form of fierce animals to a certain Christian, to alarm and threaten him. But he addressed them in this way: "I have no arms that you can fear; and if the Most High permits it, do whatever you please with me. In the meantime, however, I take the holy names of Jesus and Mary for my defense." At the very sound of these tremendous names, the earth opened, and the proud spirits cast themselves headlong into it.

St. Anselm, the great archbishop and Doctor of the Church, once declared that he himself "knew and had seen and heard many who had invoked the name of Mary in time of danger, and were immediately delivered."

St. Alphonsus Liguori

It was fitting that God should preserve Mary from original sin because he destined her to crush the head of that hellish serpent that, by seducing our first parents, brought death upon all men. This our Lord foretold to the serpent: "I will put enmity between you and the woman, and your seed and her seed. She shall crush your head" [see Gn 3:15]. But if Mary was to be that valiant woman brought into the world to conquer Lucifer, certainly it was not fitting that he should first conquer her and make her his slave. Instead, it was reasonable that she should be preserved from all stain or even momentary subjection to her opponent. The proud spirit endeavored to infect the most pure soul of this virgin with his venom, as he had already infected the whole human race.

But praised and ever blessed be God! In his infinite goodness, he endowed Mary ahead of time for this purpose with such great grace that, remaining always free from any guilt of sin, she was always able to beat down and confound the Devil's pride.

St. Alphonsus Liguori

A hermit on Mount Olivet kept a devout image of Mary in his room, and said many prayers as he knelt before it. The Devil was unable to endure such devotion to the Blessed Virgin. So he continually tormented the man with impure thoughts.

The harassment was so severe that the poor old hermit, seeing that all his prayers and penances didn't deliver him from those thoughts, one day said to the Enemy: "What have I done to you that you would torment me to death?"

At this the Devil appeared to him and replied, "You torment me much more than I do you. But if you will swear to keep it secret, I will tell you what you must give up for me to stop molesting you."

The hermit took the oath. Then the Devil said: "You must no longer pray before that image that you have in your cell."

The hermit, perplexed at this, went to consult the Abbot Theodore. The abbot told him that he was not bound by his oath, and that he must not cease to entrust himself to Mary in prayer before the image, as he had always done. The hermit obeyed, and the Devil was put to shame and conquered.

St. Alphonsus Liguori

The Devil does his utmost with sinners, so that, after they have lost the grace of God, they may also lose devotion to Mary. When Sarah saw Isaac in company with his half-brother Ishmael, who was teaching him evil habits, she wanted Abraham to drive away both Ishmael and his mother, Hagar: "Cast out this slave woman with her son" [Gn 21:10]. She was not satisfied with having the son turned out of the house, but insisted on having the mother go also. Otherwise, she thought, the son, coming to see his mother, would continue to frequent the house.

In a similar way, the Devil is not satisfied with a soul casting out Jesus Christ, unless it also casts away his mother: "Cast out this woman with her Son." Otherwise, he fears, the mother will again, by her intercession, bring back her Son. "And his fears are well grounded," says the learned scholar Angeli Pacciuchelli; "for the one who is faithful in serving the Mother of God will soon receive God himself by means of his devotion to Mary."

St. Alphonsus Liguori

"Glorious indeed, and admirable, is your name, O Mary!" exclaims St. Bonaventure. "For those who pronounce it at death need not fear all the powers of hell. The demons, on hearing that name, instantly flee, and leave the soul in peace."

"You, O Lady," says St. Germanus, "by the simple invocation of your most powerful name, give security to your servants against all the assaults of the enemy."

If only Christians were careful in their temptations to pronounce the name of Mary with confidence, they would never fall. For as Blessed Alan de la Roche remarks, "At the very sound of the words *Hail, Mary!* Satan flies, and hell trembles."

Our Blessed Lady herself revealed to St. Bridget that the enemy flees even from the most abandoned sinners—those who are consequently the furthest from God, and fully possessed by the Devil—if they will only invoke her most powerful name with a true purpose of repentance. "All demons, on hearing this name of Mary, filled with terror, leave the soul." But at the same time our Blessed Lady added: "If the soul does not repent, and wipe out its sins by sorrow, the demons almost immediately return and continue to possess it."

St. Alphonsus Liguori

A young man in Perugia, I am told, promised the Devil that if he would enable him to attain a sinful goal he had in mind, he would give him his soul. The man then gave the Devil a written contract to this effect, signed in his own blood.

When the crime had been committed, the Devil demanded that the young man keep his promise. For this purpose, he led him to the brink of a well. At the same time, the demon threatened that, if the young man didn't throw himself in, he himself would drag him, body and soul, to hell.

The wretched youth, thinking that it would be impossible to escape from the Devil's hands, climbed up to cast himself in. But terrified at the prospect of death, he told the Devil that he lacked the courage to take the leap. If the demon was determined that the youth must die, he would have to push him in.

The young man wore a scapular of the Sorrows of Mary. So the Devil said, "Take off that scapular, and then I will push you in." But the youth, discovering in the scapular the protection still promised to him by the Mother of God, refused to do so.

Finally, after a heated argument, the Devil departed, filled with humiliation. So the sinner, grateful to his sorrowful mother, went to thank her. Penitent for his sins, he presented a painting of what had taken place, as a votive offering for her altar in the church of Santa Maria la Nuova in Perugia.

St. Alphonsus Liguori

Another wonder involving Our Lady's intercession was reported by Fr. Paul Segneri in the work entitled *Christian Instructed*. The story of a young man being freed from immoral habits through devotion to her was recounted in a homily by Fr. Nicholas Zucchi in Rome. A captain in the congregation, who for many years had carried on an improper relationship with a certain woman, heard the story.

He determined that he also would practice the same devotion, so that he too might be delivered from the horrible chains that bound him as a slave of the Devil. (For it's necessary that sinners have this intention, so that the Blessed Virgin may be able to help them.) So he also gave up his wickedness and changed his life.

But there's still more. After six months, relying too much on his own strength, the captain foolishly went to pay a visit to the woman, to see whether she also were converted. But when he approached the door of the house, where he was in clear danger of falling back into sin, he was driven back by an invisible power. Suddenly he found himself far away from the house, all the way down the street, and standing in front of his own door.

Through this experience the captain was clearly made to understand that Mary had delivered him from being lost.

From this incident, we ourselves may learn a lesson: Our good mother is eager—if we entrust ourselves to her for this purpose—not only to rescue us out of a state of sin, but also to deliver us from the danger of falling back into it.

St. Alphonsus Liguori

St. Antoninus relates that there was once a sinner at enmity with God, who had a vision in which he found himself before the dread tribunal. The Devil accused him, and Mary defended him. The Enemy produced the catalog of his sins; it was thrown into the scales of divine justice, and weighed far more than all his good works. But then his great advocate, extending her sweet hand, placed it on the balance, causing it to turn in favor of her devotee. In this way she helped him understand that she would obtain his pardon if he changed his life. And so he did after the vision, and was entirely converted.

St. Alphonsus Liguori

How the demons of hell tremble at the very thought of Mary, and of her majestic name! St. Bonaventure declares: "O, how fearful is Mary to the devils!" The saint compares these enemies to those of whom Job speaks: "They dig through houses in the dark. If the morning suddenly appears, it is to them the shadow of death" [Jb 24:16–17]. Thieves go out and rob houses in the dark; but as soon as morning dawns, they flee, as if they beheld the shadow of death.

"In precisely this way," St. Bonaventure continues, "the demons enter a soul in the time of darkness"; meaning, when the soul is in the obscurity of ignorance. They dig through the house of our mind when it is in the darkness of ignorance.

But then he adds, "If suddenly they are overtaken by the dawn—that is, if the grace and mercy of Mary enters the soul—its brightness instantly dispels the darkness, and puts the hellish enemies to flight, as if they were fleeing from death." How blessed are those who always invoke the beautiful name of Mary in their conflicts with hell!

In confirmation of this reality, it was revealed to St. Bridget: "God has rendered Mary so powerful over the demons that, as often as they assault a devout believer who calls on this most Blessed Virgin for help, she at a single glance instantly terrifies them. They flee far away, preferring to have their pains redoubled rather than see themselves subject in this way to the power of Mary."

St. Alphonsus Liguori

Victory in the Name of Jesus

By invoking the name of Jesus Christ, who was crucified under Pontius Pilate, Satan is driven out of men.

St. Irenaeus

We are all inclined to sin, my children; we are idle, greedy, sensual, given to the pleasures of the flesh. We want to know everything, to learn everything, to see everything. We must watch over our mind, over our heart, and over our senses, for these are the gates by which the Devil penetrates.

See, he prowls round us incessantly; his only occupation in this world is to seek companions for himself. All our life he will lay snares for us; he will try to make us yield to temptations. We must, on our side, do all we can to defeat and resist him.

We can do nothing by ourselves, children. But we can do everything with the help of the good God. Let us pray Him to deliver us from this enemy of our salvation, or to give strength to fight against him.

With the Name of Jesus we shall overcome the demons; we shall put them to flight. With this name, though they may sometimes dare to attack us, our battles will be victories, and our victories will be crowns for heaven, all brilliant with precious stones.

St. John Vianney

The Nature of the Devil

No interval existed between the crime of the demons [their revolt against God] and its punishment. What a terrible revolution in their whole being: In their intellect, no thoughts but of crime! In their will, no love but for evil! In their abode, no other palace but hell! In their ministry, no other occupation than to pervert or torment souls! In their destiny, their end, supreme misery, and that for eternity! O terrible fall!

St. Ignatius of Loyola

Jesus said to St. Bridget: I am the Creator of all and Lord over the devils as well as over all the angels, and no one will escape My judgment. The Devil, in fact, sinned against Me in three ways: namely, through pride, through envy, and through arrogance. He was so proud indeed that he wished to be lord over Me and that I should be subject to him. He also envied Me so much that, if it were possible, he would gladly have killed Me in order to be lord himself and sit on My throne. Indeed, his own will was so dear to him that he cared nothing at all about My will as long as he could do whatever he wanted. Because of this, he fell from heaven and, no longer an angel, he became a Devil in the depths of hell.

St. Bridget of Sweden

The Devil has never made anyone or begotten anyone or created anyone; but whoever acts as the Devil acts does become in one sense a child of the Devil, as if begotten by him. The child resembles the father, not because they are literally kin, but because the child imitates the father.

St. Augustine

When the Devil is called the god of this world, it's not because he made it, but because we serve him with our worldliness.

St. Thomas Aquinas

Modern times are dominated by Satan, and will be more so in the future.

St. Maximilian Kolbe

Christ gave the Devil power over Himself so that He might be tempted and led into danger and persecuted even to the point of death, so that He might in this way liberate us from the Devil's power.

Blessed Angela of Foligno

The Power of Christian Exorcism

Come and hear the demons with your own ears. Come and see them with your own eyes when, defeated by our prayers and our spiritual flogging, and by the torture of our words, they abandon the bodies that they had possessed. . . . You will see how the demons, whom you pagans set up in high places and honor as lords, are bound by our hands and tremble under our power.

St. Cyprian of Carthage

Christ was born because of the Father's will, for the salvation of men and the ruin of demons. What you pagans see with your own eyes will convince you of this. In the entire universe and in your city of Rome there are many demon-possessed people that other exorcists, sorcerers, and magicians were unable to cure. On the other hand, we Christians were able to heal them. By commanding them in the name of Jesus Christ, who was crucified under Pontius Pilate, we reduced to impotence the demons who possessed men.

St. Justin Martyr

The Enemy's Strategies

The strategy of our Adversary can be compared to the tactics of a commander intent upon seizing and plundering a position he desires. The leader of an army will encamp, explore the fortifications and defenses of the fortress, and attack at the weakest point. In the same way, the Adversary of our human nature examines from every side all our virtues: theological, cardinal, and moral. Wherever he discovers the defenses of eternal salvation to be the weakest and most lacking, there he attacks and tries to take us by storm.

St. Ignatius of Loyola

Our Lord said to St. Catherine of Siena: I have told you that the Devil invites men to the water of death—that is, to the things he has. Then, blinding them with the pleasures and circumstances of the world, he catches them with the hook of pleasure through the lure of something good. He could catch them in no other way; they would not allow themselves to be caught if they saw that no good or pleasure for themselves could be obtained in this manner.

For the soul, by her very nature, always relishes good. Yet it is true that the soul, blinded by self-love, does not know and discern what is truly good and profitable to the soul and to the body. So the Devil, seeing them blinded by self-love, wickedly places before these souls diverse and various delights, colored so as to have the appearance of some benefit or good. He tempts each one, according to his condition, to those principal vices to which that soul seems to be most disposed.

St. Catherine of Siena

It is a mark of the Evil Spirit to take on the appearance of an angel of light. He begins by whispering thoughts that are suited to a devout soul, and ends by suggesting his own.

St. Ignatius of Loyola

Remember that the Devil never sleeps, but seeks our ruin in a thousand ways.

St. Angela Merici

The Devil never runs upon a man to seize him with his claws until he sees him on the ground, already having fallen by his own will.

St. Thomas More

There are two main deceits with which the Devil usually distances young people from virtue. The first is to make come to their mind that to serve the Lord consists in a melancholic life far from any amusement and pleasure. It's not so, dear youths. I want to teach you a Christian method of life, which is at the same time joyful and happy, pointing you to what are the true amusements and the true pleasures so you may serve the Lord and be always joyful.

St. John Bosco

Be sure that the precious oil of mildness and humility is within your heart. For one of the great deceits of the Enemy is to lead men to rest content with the external signs of these virtues without searching their inward affections. They think that because their words and looks are gentle, they themselves must be humble and mild, while in truth they are quite otherwise.

St. Francis de Sales

Before you act in any important or unusual matters upon any inspirations you believe to be from God, consult your spiritual director so he can judge whether your inspiration is true or false. For when the Enemy sees a soul ready to consent to inspirations, he often seeks to deceive it—an evil that will never happen as long as you are obedient to your director in all humility.

St. Francis de Sales

In anything that is for the service of Our Lord, the Devil tries his arts, working under the guise of holiness.

St. Teresa of Ávila

Satan has a hold both on the slanderer and on the one who listens to slander, because he has the tongue of one and the ear of the other.

St. Bernard of Clairvaux

Anxiety is the soul's greatest enemy except for sin. Internal disturbance and seditions ruin a nation and make it unfit for resisting external aggression. In the same way, when the heart is anxious and disquieted within itself, it loses the power to preserve those virtues that are already acquired, as well as the means of resisting the temptations of Satan— who never fails (as the saying goes) to fish in such troubled waters.

St. Francis de Sales

It is only towards what is good that the Enemy employs sorrow as a temptation. For inasmuch as he seeks to make sinners take delight in their sin, so he seeks to make good works onerous to those who are righteous. And as he can lead the one to evil only by making it seem agreeable, so can he deter the other from what is good only by making it seem disagreeable. Satan delights in sadness and melancholy, since he himself is sad and melancholy, and will be so for all eternity—a condition he wants everyone else to share with him. . . .

Vigorously check the inclination to sadness. Even though you may seem to do everything coldly, sadly, and without fervor, go on all the same. For the Enemy would gladly enfeeble our good works by sadness; and when he finds that we will not discontinue them, and that they are all the more meritorious through resistance, he will cease to annoy us.

St. Francis de Sales

When the sly demon, after using many devices, fails to hinder the prayer of the diligent, he desists for a little while. But when the man has finished his prayers, the demon takes his revenge.

He either fires the man's anger and thus destroys the good condition produced by prayer, or he excites an impulse toward some animal pleasure and thus mocks the man's mind.

St. Nilus of Sinai

Our infernal Enemy observes, with malicious intention, the stamp of our conscience—whether it is too sensitive or too relaxed. If too sensitive, he tries to make it even more susceptible to scruples. He endeavors to reduce it to the last degree of trouble and anguish, so as to stop its progress in the spiritual life.

To this timid Christian, who never consents to any sin either mortal or venial, and who dreads even the appearance of a voluntary fault, the Enemy cannot dangle the bait of a real sin. So instead he presents an imaginary fault as a frightful phantom. Sin will appear to him in a trifling word, a thought that only crossed his mind, and so on.

On the other hand, if the Enemy finds in someone a relaxed conscience, he studies to make it even more so. Because this soul is not afraid of venial sin, he familiarizes it, little by little, with mortal sin. And day by day he weakens the horror of such sin in the eyes of that soul.

St. Ignatius of Loyola

Dealing With the Devil

God said to St. Bridget: The Devil and I do struggle, in that we both desire souls as bridegrooms desire their brides. For I desire souls in order to give them eternal joy and honor, but the Devil desires souls to give them eternal horror and sorrow.

St. Bridget of Sweden

Whenever my enemy provokes me to combat, I try to behave like a soldier.

St. Thérèse of Lisieux

Great courage is required in spiritual warfare.

St. Teresa of Ávila

Draw near to God, and Satan will flee from you.

St. Ephraem the Syrian

God gives the Devil power against us in two modes: either for punishment when we sin, or for glory when we are tested.

St. Cyprian of Carthage

The soul possesses freedom; and though the Devil can make suggestions, he doesn't have the power to compel you against your will.

St. Cyril of Jerusalem

Committing sin makes us strangers to God and partners with the Devil.

St. Basil the Great

Listen: There are two things the Devil is deathly afraid of: *fervent Communions and frequent visits to the Blessed Sacrament.*

Do you want Our Lord to grant you *many* graces? Visit him *often.*

Do you want Him to grant you *only* a few? Visit Him only *seldom.*

Do you want the Devil to *attack you? Rarely* visit the Blessed Sacrament.

Do you want the Devil to *flee from* you? Visit Jesus *often.*

Do you want to *overcome* the Devil? Take refuge *at Jesus' feet.*

Do you want *to be overcome* by the Devil? Give up visiting Jesus.

Visiting the Blessed Sacrament is essential, my dear boys, if you want to overcome the Devil. Therefore, make frequent visits to Jesus. If you do that, the Devil will never prevail against you.

St. John Bosco

The Devil's snare can't catch you unless you're already nibbling on the Devil's bait.

St. Ambrose of Milan

To sin is human, but to persist in sin is devilish.

St. Catherine of Siena

Repentance is returning from the unnatural to the natural state, from the Devil to God, through discipline and effort.

St. John the Damascene

Hence the Lord has said that he who has faith the size of a mustard seed can move a mountain by a word of command; that is, he can destroy the Devil's dominion over us and remove it from its foundation.

St. Maximus the Confessor

However great may be the temptation, if we know how to use the weapon of prayer well, we shall come off as conquerors at last, for prayer is more powerful than all the demons. He who is attacked by the spirits of darkness needs only to apply himself vigorously to prayer, and he will beat them back with great success.

St. Bernard of Clairvaux

Do not oppose head-on the thoughts that the Enemy sows in your mind. Instead, cut off all conversation with them by prayer to God.

St. Isaak of Syria

We have been called to heal wounds, to unite what has fallen apart, and to bring home those who have lost their way. Many who may seem to us to be children of the Devil will still become Christ's disciples.

St. Francis of Assisi

The soul that is united with God is feared by the Devil as if it were God Himself.

St. John of the Cross

Let the Enemy rage at the gate, let him knock, let him push, let him cry, let him howl, let him do worse; we know for certain that he cannot enter, save by the door of our consent.

St. Francis de Sales

I don't understand those fears that make us cry, "The Devil! The Devil!" when we can say, "God! God!"

St. Teresa of Ávila

In the Eucharist, Christ has given to those who desire Him the ability not only to see Him, but even to touch Him, eat Him, fix their teeth in His flesh, and embrace Him, to satisfy all their love. For this reason, we must return from that Table like lions breathing fire, having become terrifying to the Devil. We must be thinking about Christ our Head, and about the love He's shown to us.

St. John Chrysostom

Be eager to gather more frequently to give thanks to God in the Eucharist and for His glory. For when we meet this way, the forces of Satan are nullified, and his destructive power is cancelled in the harmony of your faith.

St. Ignatius of Antioch

If we are hindered by some particular vice, we should as far as possible strive to cultivate the opposite virtue, making all things tend to it. For by this means we shall subdue the Enemy, and not cease to advance in all virtue.

St. Francis de Sales

The way to overcome the Devil when he excites feelings of hatred for those who injure us is to pray immediately for their conversion.

St. John Vianney

The principal trap that the Devil sets for young people is idleness. This is a fatal source of all evil. Do not let there be any doubt in your mind that we are born to work, and when we don't, we're out of our element and in great danger of offending God. . . . First tell the Devil to rest, and then I'll rest, too.

St. John Bosco

Before we can receive the grace of God into our hearts they must be thoroughly empty of all self-glory. The falcon has a peculiar property of frightening away birds of prey with its looks and cries. Consequently, the dove seeks it beyond all other birds, and lives fearlessly in its neighborhood.

In a similar way, humility repulses Satan and preserves in us the gifts and graces of the Holy Spirit. For this reason all the saints, and especially the King of saints and His mother, have always honored and cherished this virtue above all others.

St. Francis de Sales

Humility is the only virtue no demon can imitate.

St. John Climacus

We crush the head of the Serpent when we scorn and trample underfoot the glory of the world, the praises, the vanities, and all the other pomps of pride.

St. Marie of the Incarnation

When invisible and sinful desires are overcome, we then overcome the unseen power of our Enemy. By overcoming within ourselves the inordinate love for things of this world, we are necessarily, within ourselves, overcoming the one who rules within man by these sinful desires.

St. Augustine

Job was turned over to the Devil to be tempted so that, by withstanding the test, Job would become a torment to the Devil.

St. Augustine

Prayer, without a doubt, is the most powerful weapon the Lord gives us to conquer evil, but we must really put ourselves into the prayer. It is not enough just to say the words; it must come from the heart. And also prayer needs to be continuous. We must pray no matter what kind of situation we find ourselves in. The warfare in which we are engaged is ongoing, so our prayer must be ongoing as well.

St. Alphonsus Liguori

If you are able to fast, you will do well to observe some abstinence beyond what is enjoined by the Church. For in addition to the ordinary benefits of fasting—namely, lifting up the mind, subduing the flesh, strengthening virtue, and earning an eternal recompense—it is a great matter to be able to command our tastes and inclinations, and to keep the body and its appetites subject to the law of the spirit. And even if we do not fast to any great extent, Satan is the more afraid of those who, he is aware, know how to fast.

St. Francis de Sales

A man who is deeply wounded in his heart by provocation and abuse shows thereby that deep in himself he harbors the old Serpent. If he bears the blows in silence and answers with great humility, he will render the Serpent weak or will kill it altogether. But if he argues with bitterness or speaks with arrogance, he will give the Serpent an added strength to pour poison into his heart and mercilessly to devour his entrails.

St. Simeon the New Theologian

In times of spiritual coldness and laziness, imagine in your heart those times in the past when you were full of zeal and solicitude in all things, even the smallest. Remember your past efforts and the energy with which you opposed those who wanted to obstruct your progress. These recollections will reawaken your soul from its deep sleep, will invest it once more with the fire of zeal, will raise it, as it were, from the dead, and will make it engage in an ardent struggle against the Devil and sin, thus being restored to its former height.

St. Isaak of Syria

To free a man who is a bodily captive in the hands of the barbarians is a noble deed. But to free a soul from the slavery of Satan is greater than to deliver all who are in bodily slavery.

St. John Eudes

If Christ is with us, who can be against us? You can fight with confidence when you are sure of victory. With Christ and for Christ, victory is certain.

St. Bernard of Clairvaux

If we really desire to enter into this spiritual combat on the same terms as the Apostle [2 Tm 4:7], let us concentrate our every effort at dominating this unclean spirit [of lust] by placing our confidence not in our own forces but in the help of God. Human effort will never be able to win here. For the soul will be attacked by this vice as long as it does not recognize that it is in a war beyond its powers and that it cannot obtain victory by its own effort unless it is shored up by the help and protection of the Lord.

St. John Cassian

Sometimes, the Devil inspires souls with an inordinate zeal for a certain virtue or some special pious exercise, so that they will be motivated in its practice by passion. Or again, he permits them to become discouraged so that they will neglect everything because they are wearied and disgusted. It is necessary to overcome that one snare as well as the other.

St. Catherine of Bologna

These cursed spirits torment me quite frequently, but they do not frighten me in the least. For I am convinced that they cannot move except by God's permission.

Let this be known well: Every time we make the demons the object of our contempt, they lose their strength, and the soul acquires a greater superiority over them. They have no power except against cowardly souls who surrender their weapons.

St. Teresa of Ávila

Once we have exposed the infernal Serpent—when, by the evil results to which his insinuations always tend, we have discovered his diabolical purpose—then this strategy is very useful: Go over again in spirit the way by which the Tempter led us. Analyze the steps of the plot he had so carefully laid.

Note the deceptive pretexts through which he began to make us listen to him. Consider how he succeeded, little by little, in changing that pure taste, that spiritual sweetness, that perfect serenity we enjoyed before. See how he endeavored to inject his venom into the soul.

This study of his hateful maneuvers will render us more capable of escaping them in the future.

St. Ignatius of Loyola

God Watches Us Fight

Men are trained and prepared for secular contests, and they account it a great mark of honor if they happen to be crowned in the sight of the people and the presence of the emperor. But consider this sublime and mighty contest, glorious with the prize of a heavenly crown, in which God beholds us contending. Extending His vision over those whom He has promised to make sons, He delights in beholding our struggle.

God beholds us fighting and engaging in the conflict of faith; His angels behold us. Christ also beholds us. How great the dignity of glory, how great the happiness, to engage in combat in the presence of God, and to be crowned by Christ our Judge! Let's arm ourselves, most beloved brothers, with all our might, and be prepared for the contest with minds undefiled, with faith entire, and devoted courage.

St. Cyprian

The Our Father Is a Battle Cry

In the Our Father, Christ has just spoken of the Evil One, placing us on alert before the battle, reminding us of our enemy, and keeping us from negligence. Now He goes on to encourage us and raise our spirits by recognizing the King who leads us into the field, pointing to Him as the One who is more powerful than all. Christ says, "For the kingdom, the power, and the glory are Yours" [see Mt 6:13].

Doesn't it follow, then, that if the kingdom belongs to God, we should fear no one? For no one can withstand Him or tear apart His empire. When Christ says, "The kingdom is Yours," He shows us that even the enemy warring against us has been brought into subjection to God.

The Devil may seem still to be fighting against us, but God is only permitting it for now. After all, he too is one of God's servants, though a corrupt and guilty one. He would not dare fight any of his fellow servants if he had not first received permission from above.

"The power is Yours," Christ says. For this reason, no matter how many forms your weakness may take, you may still rightly be confident in the battle. You have the kind of Sovereign who's able to accomplish everything necessary that concerns you, and to do it with ease.

"The glory is Yours." Not only can God free you from the dangers you face; He can also make you glorious and outstanding in battle. His power is great and His glory is beyond telling—they are both limitless and never come to an end. See how He has in every way anointed you, His champion, and surrounded you with confidence?

St. John Chrysostom

The Devil Is Like a Siege Force

Beloved brothers and sisters, we must strive with all our strength to repel the Enemy of our souls, with full attention and vigilance, as he rages and aims his darts against every part of us that can be assaulted and wounded. This is what the Apostle Peter, in his epistle, warns and teaches us about, saying: "Be sober, be watchful. Your adversary the Devil prowls around like a roaring lion, seeking someone to devour" [1 Pt 5:8].

He circles around each of us. Like an army coming against those besieged in a city, he examines the city walls, looking for places that are less firm, less trustworthy. When the weaknesses are found, the siege forces break through them and penetrate to the inside.

The Enemy presents to the eyes seductive images and easy pleasures, so he can destroy chastity through the sense of sight. He tempts the ears with seductive music, so that by hearing these sweet sounds, the soul relaxes its guard and loses strength. He provokes the tongue by rebukes. He instigates the hand to do evil through exasperating wrongs that provoke recklessness leading to murder.

To induce someone to cheat, he presents the lure of dishonest gains. To take the soul captive by money, he heaps together hoards of it that will work mischief. He promises earthly honors so that he can deprive us of heavenly ones.

He makes a show of false things, so that he can steal away the true ones. And when he can't deceive through stealth, he threatens explicitly and openly, holding out the fear of violent persecution to vanquish God's servants. He's always restless and always hostile, crafty in peace and fierce in persecution.

For these reasons, beloved brothers and sisters, the mind ought to stand arrayed and armed against all the Devil's deceiving snares and open threats, as ever-ready to repel as the foe is ever-ready to attack.

St. Cyprian of Carthage

God Turned the Tables on the Devil!

Hades and the Devil have been pillaged, stripped of their ancient armor, robbed of their special power. And just as the giant Goliath had his head cut off with his own sword, so also has the Devil, the father of death, been put to rout through the death of Christ. He finds that the very same weapon he used to wield as the ready tool of his deceit has now become the mighty instrument of his own destruction.

We might put it this way: The Devil went fishing and cast his line and hook to catch yet another man in death. But the Man he caught this time was Christ, whose divine nature was hidden within His human nature.

So this time, the Devil himself was baited: When he hooked Christ's human nature, he himself was hooked by Christ's divine nature. The Devil thought he was the fisherman, but instead he became the catch.

For this reason, the martyrs leap upon the head of that dragon the Devil, and look with disdain on every kind of torment.

St. Gregory Thaumaturgus

Shun the Devil's False Promises

The Devil didn't deal out temptations to Our Lord only. He brings these evil schemes of his to bear on each of Jesus' servants—and not just on the mountain or in the wilderness or when we're by ourselves. No, he comes after us in the city as well, in the marketplaces, in courts of justice. He tempts us by means of others, even our own relatives.

So what must we do? We must disbelieve him altogether, and close our ears against him, and hate his flattery. And when he tries to tempt us further by offering us even more, then we should shun him all the more.

Remember the example of Eve: When the Devil was lifting her up the highest with hopes—telling her she could become like God—that's when he cast her down and did her the greatest evils. Yes, for he is an implacable enemy, and he's taken up against us the kind of war that will never allow for a treaty.

We aren't as intent on gaining our own salvation as he is intent on achieving our ruin. So we must shun him, not with words only, but also with works; not in mind only, but also in deed. We must do none of the things that he approves, for in that way we'll do all those things that God approves.

Yes, for the Devil also makes many promises, not so that he may give to us, but so that he may take away from us. He promises us plunder, so that he may deprive us of the kingdom of God and of righteousness. He sets out treasures in the earth as snares and traps, so that he may deprive us both of these and of the treasures in heaven. He would have us be rich in this life, so that we may not be rich in the next.

St. John Chrysostom

Empty Consolations From the Devil

Some people, when they reflect on the goodness of God and the passion of Christ, are powerfully moved to sighs, tears, prayers, and other devout actions, so that you might suppose their hearts were seized with a very fervent devotion. But when they are tested we find that they are like the passing rains of a hot summer, which may fall heavily on the earth, but do not penetrate it, and bring forth only mushrooms.

In the same way, these tears and emotions in a corrupt heart do not penetrate it and are altogether fruitless. For these unhappy people would not give up a penny of their unjustly acquired wealth or renounce one of their perverse affections, nor would they endure the slightest suffering in the service of that Savior over whom they have wept.

Their good impulses are like spiritual mushrooms. Not only are they a false devotion, but too often they are actually the deep wiles of Satan. While he amuses souls with such empty consolations, he induces them to remain satisfied with them instead of seeking true and solid devotion, which consists in a constant, resolute, prompt, and active will to carry out what we know to be pleasing to God.

St. Francis de Sales

The Devil Fears Those Who Pray

My dear brothers and sisters, not only is prayer very powerful; even more, it's of the utmost necessity for overcoming the enemies of our salvation. Look at all the saints: They weren't content with watching and fighting to overcome the enemies of their salvation and with keeping well away from all that could offer them temptation. They passed their whole lives in prayer, not only the day, but very often the whole night as well.

Yes, my dear children, we watch over ourselves and all the motions of our hearts in vain, and in vain we avoid temptation, if we don't pray. If we don't continually resort to prayer, all our other ways will be of no use at all to us, and we'll be overcome.

We won't find any sinner converted without turning to prayer. We won't find one persevering without depending heavily on prayer. Nor will we ever find a Christian who ends up damned whose downfall didn't begin with a lack of prayer.

We can see, too, how much the Devil fears those who pray, since there's not a moment of the day when he tempts us more than when we're at prayer. He does everything he possibly can to prevent us from praying. When the Devil wants to make someone lose his soul, he starts out by inspiring in him a profound distaste for prayer. However good a Christian he may be, if the Devil succeeds in making him either say his prayers badly or neglect them altogether, he's certain to have that person for himself.

Yes, my dear brothers and sisters, from the moment that we neglect to pray, we move with big steps toward hell. We'll never return to God if we don't resort to prayer.

St. John Vianney

Holy Water Puts Demons to Flight

I know by frequent experience that there is nothing that puts the demons to flight like holy water. They run away before the Sign of the Cross as well, but they return immediately: Great, then, must be the power of holy water.

As for me, my soul is conscious of a special and most distinct consolation whenever I take it. Indeed, I feel almost always a certain refreshing that I cannot describe, together with an inward joy that comforts my whole soul. This is no fancy, nor a thing that has occurred once only; for it has happened very often, and I have watched it very carefully.

I may compare what I feel with what happens to a person who is very hot, and very thirsty, drinking a cup of cold water. His whole being is refreshed. I consider that everything ordained by the Church is very important; and I have a joy in considering that the words of the Church are so mighty that they endow water with power, so that there becomes a great difference between holy water and water that has never been blessed.

St. Teresa of Ávila

The Sign of the Cross

The Sign of the Cross is the most terrible weapon against the Devil. For this reason, the Church displays images of the Cross so that we can have it continually in front of our minds to recall to us just what our souls are worth and what they cost Jesus Christ. For the same reason, the Church wants us to make the Sign of the Cross ourselves at every juncture of our day: when we go to bed, when we awaken during the night, when we get up, when we begin any action, and above all when we're tempted.

Fill your children, my dear brethren, with the greatest respect for the Cross, and always have a blessed cross on yourselves. Respect for the Cross will protect you against the Devil, from the vengeance of heaven, and from all danger.

St. John Vianney

The Snare of Spiritual Counterfeits

When I was still casting about spiritually, whom could I find to reconcile me to You, Lord? Was I to ask spirits for help? By what prayer? By what rituals?

Many who strive to return to You, but are unable to do so on their own, have tried this path, I am told. They have fallen into a craving for strange visions. And they have been rewarded with delusions.

Being arrogant, they sought You with a pride in what they learned, puffing out their chests instead of beating them in penance. And so by a likeness in heart, they drew themselves to the demonic princes of the air, their conspirators and companions in pride. But they were deceived by those spirits through the power of magic.

They thought they were looking for You, Lord. But they found the Devil instead, who took on the appearance of an angel of light.

St. Augustine

How wide is the scope of inquisitiveness—the foolish desire to know everything. It's at work in spectacles, in theaters, in satanic rites, in the magical arts, in dealings with darkness. It's none other than idle curiosity.

St. Augustine

Discerning Private Revelations

I look upon it as a most certain truth, that the Devil will never deceive, and that God will not allow him to deceive, the soul that has no confidence whatever in itself; the soul that is strong in faith and resolved to undergo a thousand deaths for any one article of the creed; the soul that, in its love of the faith, infused by God once for all—a faith living and strong—always labors, seeking for further light on this side and on that, to mold itself on the teaching of the Church, as one already deeply grounded in the truth. Even if that soul saw the heavens open, no imaginable "revelation" could make it swerve in any degree from the doctrine of the Church. . . .

As far as I can see, and by experience understand, whatever claims to come from God should be accepted only in as far as it agrees with the Sacred Scriptures. But if I should find that a seeming "revelation" contradicts Scripture even a little, then no matter how convinced I may have been before that it came from God—however deep that conviction may have been—I will be incomparably more convinced now that it comes from Satan.

In this case, there is no need to ask for signs to confirm the authenticity of the alleged revelation, nor to attempt to discern from which spirit it proceeds. This contradiction of

Scripture is so clear a sign of the Devil's presence, that if all the world were to assure me that the alleged revelation came from God, I would not believe it.

St. Teresa of Ávila

Why God Allows the Devil to Tempt Us

Our Lord said to St. Catherine of Siena: I've appointed the Devil to tempt and to trouble My creatures in this life. I've done this, not so that My creatures will be overcome, but so that *they* may overcome, proving their virtue and receiving from Me the glory of victory. And no one should fear any battle or temptation of the Devil that may come to him, because I've made My creatures strong, and I've given them strength of will, fortified in the blood of My Son.

Neither the Devil nor any other creature can control this free will, because it's yours, given to you by Me. By your own choice, then, you can hold it or let go of it as you please. It's a weapon, and if you place it in the hands of the Devil, it right away becomes a knife that he'll use to stab and kill you.

On the other hand, if you don't place this knife that is your will into the hands of the Devil—that is, if you don't consent to his temptations and harassments—you will never be injured by the guilt of sin in any temptation. Instead, you'll actually be strengthened by the temptation, as long as you open the eyes of your mind to see My love, and to understand why I allowed you to be tempted: so you could develop virtue by having it proved.

My love permits these temptations, for the Devil is weak. He can do nothing by himself unless I allow him. So I let him tempt you because I love you, not because I hate you. I want you to conquer, not to be conquered, and to come to a perfect knowledge of yourself and of Me.

St. Catherine of Siena

The Devil Tempts Us Especially When We're Alone

"Then Jesus was led up by the Spirit into the wilderness to be tempted by the Devil" [Mt 4:1]. See where the Spirit led Him up, when He had come upon Him in His baptism: not into a city and a public place, but into a wilderness.

Jesus' intention was to have the Devil come after Him. So He gave him an opportunity to tempt Him not only through His hunger, but also through the kind of place where He was. For the Devil most especially assaults us when he sees us left alone, all by ourselves.

In this way he also set his trap for the first woman, Eve, in the beginning. He caught her alone and found her apart from her husband.

It's the same with us: When the Devil sees us with others and banded together, he's not as confident of himself, and he makes no attack. For this reason we have the greatest need to be flocking together continually, so that we won't be open to the Devil's attacks.

So the Devil found Jesus alone in the wilderness, and in the wilderness off the beaten path—for that's what the Gospel of Mark tells us when it says that Jesus "was with the wild beasts" [Mk 1:13]. See, then, how craftily and wickedly the Devil draws near, and notice what kind of opportunity he's waiting for.

St. John Chrysostom

Strength in the Eucharist

What does Jesus Christ do in the Eucharist? It is God who, as our Savior, offers Himself each day for us to His Father's justice. If you are in difficulties and sorrows, He will comfort and relieve you. If you are sick, He will either cure you or give you strength to suffer so as to merit heaven. If the Devil, the world, and the flesh are making war upon you, He will give you the weapons with which to fight, to resist, and to

win victory. If you are poor, He will enrich you with all sorts
of riches for time and eternity. Let us open the door of His
Sacred Heart, worthy to be adored, and be wrapped about
for an instant by the flames of His love—and we shall see
what a God who loves us can do.

St. John Vianney

O living Host, my one and only Strength, Fountain of love
and mercy, embrace the whole world, and fortify faint souls!

St. Faustina Kowalska

Resisting Temptation

If in Christ we have been tempted, in Him we overcome
the Devil. Do you think only of Christ's temptations and
fail to think of His victory? See yourself as tempted in
Him, and see yourself as victorious in Him. He could
have kept the Devil away from Himself, but if He had not
been tempted He could not teach you how to triumph
over temptation.

St. Augustine

As the pilot of a vessel is tried in the storm; as the wrestler
is tried in the ring, the soldier in the battle, and the hero in
adversity: so is the Christian tried in temptation.

St. Basil the Great

Whatever good is to be attained, struggle is necessary. So
don't fear temptations, but rejoice in them, for they lead to
achievement. God helps and protects you.

St. Barsanuphius of Gaza

It is necessary that temptations should happen. For who will
be crowned except the one who will have lawfully fought?
And how will a man fight if there is no one to attack him?

St. Bernard of Clairvaux

The greatest of all evils is not to be tempted, because then there are grounds for believing that the Devil looks upon us as his property.

St. John Vianney

In your strife with the Devil, you have for spectators the angels and the Lord of angels.

St. Ephraem the Syrian

The soul can, by her free will, make a choice either of good or evil, according to how it pleases her will. So great is this liberty that we have, and so strong has this liberty been made by virtue of Christ's glorious blood, that no demon or creature can constrain us to one smallest fault without our free consent.

St. Catherine of Siena

The demons either tempt us themselves or incite against us people who have no fear of God. They tempt us themselves when we go into seclusion from men, as the Lord was tempted in the wilderness. They tempt through people when we have dealings with them, again as they tested the Lord through the Pharisees. But if we keep our eyes fixed on our example, that is, the Lord, we shall repulse them alike in each case.

St. Maximus the Confessor

The thought comes to me to commit a mortal sin. I resist that thought immediately, and it is conquered. If the same evil thought comes to me and I resist it, and it returns again and again, yet I continue to resist it until it is vanquished, the second way is even more meritorious than the first.

He who remembers the presence of God is less open to other thoughts, especially bad thoughts. . . . In two ways the presence of God is an antidote against sin: first, because God sees us, and second, because we see God.

St. Ignatius of Loyola

The Devil tempts so that he may ruin; God tests so that He may crown.

St. Ambrose of Milan

For the Devil does not seduce or influence anyone, unless he finds him ready in some way similar to himself. He finds him coveting something, for example, and greed opens the door for the Devil's suggestion to enter.

St. Augustine

The Tempter, ever on the lookout, wages war most violently against those he sees most careful to avoid sin.

Pope St. Leo the Great

When tempted, invoke your guardian angel. Ignore the Devil and do not be afraid of him. He trembles and flees at the sight of your guardian angel.

St. John Bosco

Close your ears to the whisperings of hell and bravely oppose its onslaughts.

St. Clare of Assisi

When evil thoughts come into your heart, dash them at once on the rock of Christ and disclose them to your spiritual father.

St. Benedict

Occupy your minds with good thoughts, or the Enemy will fill them with bad ones. Unoccupied, they cannot be.

St. Thomas More

When an evil thought is presented to the mind, we must immediately endeavor to turn our thoughts to God, or to something that is indifferent. But the first rule is this:

Instantly invoke the names of Jesus and Mary, and continue to invoke them until the temptation ceases.

St. Alphonsus Liguori

Note well Lucifer's tricks, and the three ordinary degrees of temptation. First, he catches souls by the love of riches; next, he throws them into the paths of ambition; then, from ambition to pride—a bottomless abyss, from which all vices rise as from their fount. See with what patience and acts of zeal the ministers of Lucifer execute the task imposed on them by their master, how they make everything lead to the one goal: the ruin of souls—defects of the understanding, inclinations of the heart, the character, the passions, the habits, the faults, even the virtues and divine graces.

Finally, contemplate the success of hell in its undertaking: how many fools are taken in these snares every day; how many blindly throw themselves in; how many who, not content to allow themselves to be seduced, seek also to seduce their brethren. Look at yourself. Be astonished at having given way so often and so easily to the temptations of the Enemy. Weep over your folly and your past weakness, and resolve to be wiser and more courageous for the future.

St. Ignatius of Loyola

Do not confer with the Enemy. Do not say, "I will listen to him, but not obey him, I will open my ears, but close my heart to him." Rather be strict in such things. The heart and the ears are closely connected, and as it is impossible to stop a torrent in its course down the mountainside, so is it to defend the heart from what we allow into our ears.

St. Francis de Sales

He did not say: You will not be troubled; you will not be tempted; you will not be distressed. But He said: You will not be overcome.

Blessed Julian of Norwich

Never seek temptations. It is presumptuous and rash to do so. But prepare your heart to await them with courage and to defend itself when they do come.

St. Francis de Sales

All the temptations of hell cannot stain a soul that does not love them.

St. Francis de Sales

To defend his purity, St. Francis of Assisi rolled in the snow, St. Benedict threw himself into a thorn bush, and St. Bernard plunged into an icy pond. And you? What have you done?

St. Josemaría Escrivá

INDEX

tree of the knowledge of good and
evil, 7
trials and afflictions, embracing, 95
truffle-eater, evil spirit calling John
Vianney as, 148
"The Two Standards," 110

unclean spirits: attempting to
convince Catherine she was one
of them, 102–3; dominating, 218.
See also demon(s)
University of St. Mark, 136

Vade retro satana ("Get back,
Satan!"), 51
vainglory: Francis wanting to avoid,
86–87; Gemma not seduced by,
163
vanity, prompting Gemma to, 163
Velázquez, Anna, 136
venial sin, 212
Vianney, St. John, 143–54, 206;
birth and childhood of, 144;
blessing a demonic woman, 153;
curing demonic possession, 154;
on dealing with the Devil, 216;
on Devil fearing those who pray,
224–25; frightened by demonic
activity, 147; haunted by fear of
being eternally lost, 147; hearing
sounds with no human origin,
147; manifestations increasingly
bizarre, 149–50; military career,
144; on resisting temptation,
231; on the Sign of the Cross,
226; on strength in the Eucharist, 229–30; studies of, 144–45;
tormented by thoughts of future

destiny, 147; treated as a false
visionary, 151
vice: Benedict freed from, 46; hindered by some particular, 215
victim souls, 156–57, 171, 175
victory certain with Christ, 218
Viking raiders, 61
violence of Satan against Gemma,
160
violent persecution, fear of, 222
virginity consecrated to Christ,
93
virtue, zeal for, 127
Visigoths, 43
visions: craving for strange, 226; of
Ignatius, 106–7
Viti, Blessed Mary Fortunata,
195

war in heaven becoming a war on
earth, 6
water, endowing with power, 130,
225
weaknesses, Devil finding, 221
West, lapsing into a post-Christian
condition, 183
western Europe, of the fourteenth
century, 92
wilderness: combat in, 55–57; filled
with monks, 40–42; life in, as
more focused on God, 41
Word. *See* Jesus Christ
work, 216
worldliness, 72, 207
world of woe, 8

zeal, 218
Zucchi, Fr. Nicholas, 204

 TAN · BOOKS

TAN Books is the Publisher You Can Trust With Your Faith.

TAN Books was founded in 1967 to preserve the spiritual, intellectual, and liturgical traditions of the Catholic Church. At a critical moment in history TAN kept alive the great classics of the Faith and drew many to the Church. In 2008 TAN was acquired by Saint Benedict Press. Today TAN continues to teach and defend the Faith to a new generation of readers.

TAN publishes more than 600 booklets, Bibles, and books. Popular subject areas include theology and doctrine, prayer and the supernatural, history, biography, and the lives of the saints. TAN's line of educational and homeschooling resources is featured at TANHomeschool.com.

TAN publishes under several imprints, including TAN, Neumann Press, ACS Books, and the Confraternity of the Precious Blood. Sister imprints include Saint Benedict Press, Catholic Courses, and Catholic Scripture Study International.

**For more information about TAN,
or to request a free catalog, visit
TANBooks.com**

**Or call us toll-free at
(800) 437-5876**

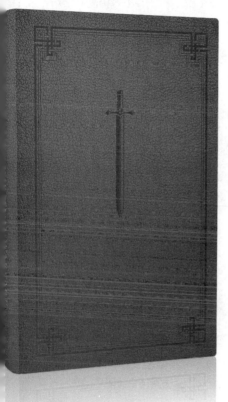

Manual for Spiritual Warfare

Paul Thigpen, Ph.D.

A fierce war rages for your soul. Are you ready for battle?

Like it or not, you are at war. It's a spiritual battle with crucial consequences in your everyday life — and its outcome will determine your eternal destiny. You must engage the Enemy. And as you fight, you need a *Manual for Spiritual Warfare*.

978-1-61890-653-3 • Premium UltraSoft

Part One, "Preparing for Battle," answers these critical questions:

Who is Satan?

What powers does he have?

What are his typical strategies?

Who fights him alongside us in battle?

What spiritual weapons and armor do we possess?

How do we keep the Enemy out of our camp?

Part Two, "Aids in Battle," provides you these essential resources:

- Teaching about spiritual warfare from Scripture and Church documents
- Scripture verses for battle
- Wisdom and inspiration from saints who fought Satan
- Prayers for protection, deliverance, and victory
- Rosary meditations, hymns, and other devotions for spiritual combat

St. Paul urges us to "fight the good fight of the faith" (1 Tim 6:12). Take this *Manual for Spiritual Warfare* with you into battle.

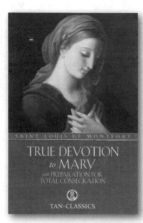

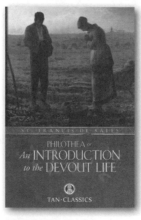
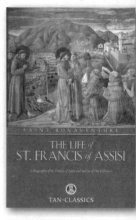

978-0-89555-153-5

978-0-89555-149-8

978-0-89555-199-3

The collection includes distinguished spiritual works of
the saints, philosophical treatises and famous biographies.

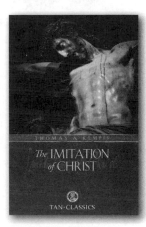

978-0-89555-226-6

978-0-89555-152-8

978-0-89555-225-9

Visit us at TANBooks.com

Spread the Faith with . . .

TAN·BOOKS

A Division of Saint Benedict Press, LLC

TAN books are powerful tools for evangelization. They lift the mind to God and change lives. Millions of readers have found in TAN books and booklets an effective way to teach and defend the Faith, soften hearts, and grow in prayer and holiness of life.

Throughout history the faithful have distributed Catholic literature and sacramentals to save souls. St. Francis de Sales passed out his own pamphlets to win back those who had abandoned the Faith. Countless others have distributed the Miraculous Medal to prompt conversions and inspire deeper devotion to God. Our customers use TAN books in that same spirit.

If you have been helped by this or another TAN title, share it with others. Become a TAN Missionary and share our life changing books and booklets with your family, friends and community. We'll help by providing special discounts for books and booklets purchased in quantity for purposes of evangelization. Write or call us for additional details.

TAN Books
Attn: TAN Missionaries Department
PO Box 410487
Charlotte, NC 28241

Toll-free (800) 437-5876
missionaries@TANBooks.com